Spirit of Qiw

Mireille Westerduin

Global Doodle Gems Volume 14
"The Ultimate International Coloring Book...an epic Collection from Artists around the World!"

Esther Lafiebre

Marie-Eve Klein colored by Sophie Guillaumot

Irina Sergeeva colored by Diane Blair

Jane Levi colored by CreaSam

Joann Sands

M. Lin

Asma Zergui

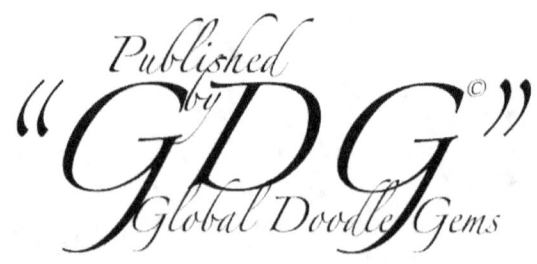

Share your colored versions with us ! We love seeing your results and hearing from you we are social !

The Official FB book page, stay on top of what we have in the works !
www.facebook.com/globaldoodlegems
The Community group, share your colored pages, meet the artists, enjoy exclusive freebies, take part in community Charity books and so much more......
www.facebook.com/groups/globaldoodlegems/
Follow us on Twitter.... @GlobalDoodlegem
We are on Instagram too
@globaldoodlegems for instagram
...and if you are not social like that we have a blog
globaldoodlegems.wordpress.com

Copyright © 2016 Global Doodle Gems
All rights are reserved by Global Doodle Gems.
Duplication of pages for personal use are allowed. You are invited to color the pages then scan/post your coloured versions to social networks, mentioning the book title and author/artist (Global Doodle Gems).
All artwork and images are protected by copyright laws. This book or any portion thereof may not, otherwise, be reproduced and/or distributed or transmitted without the express written permission of the artist/publisher of Global Doodle Gems.
All of us from the Global Doodle Gems wish you a colortastic time and look forward to seeing your wonderful color results online !

Contributing Artists

1. Esther Lafiebre
2. Spirit of Qiw
3. Marie-Eve Klein
4. Jane Levi
5. Irina Sergeeva
6. Joann Sands
7. Fabienne Tosi
8. Asma Zergui
9. Mireille Westerduin
10. M. Lin

Chapter 1
Esther Lafiebre
Canarias, Spain

Facebook .esther lafiebre
Instagram estherlafiebre

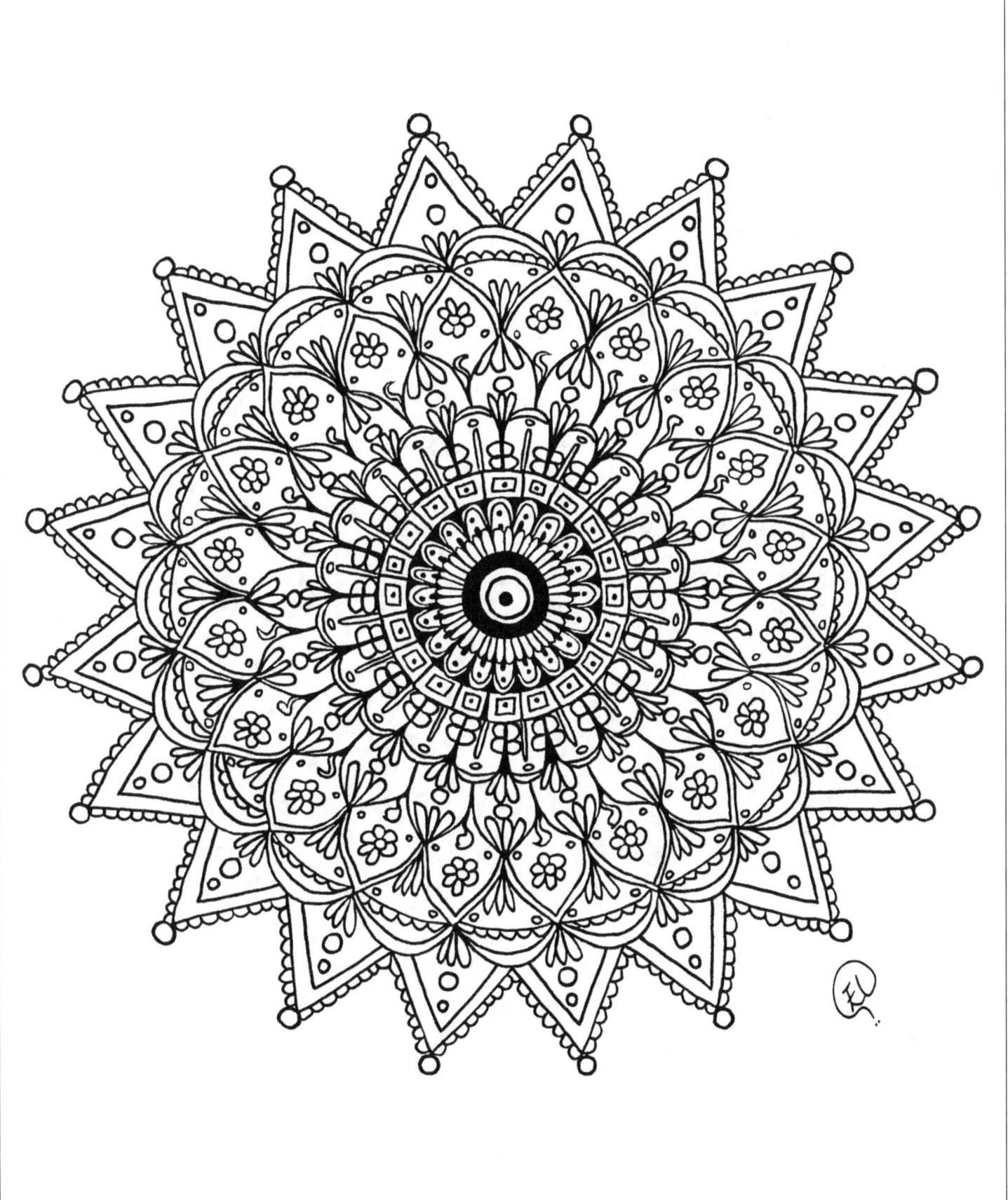

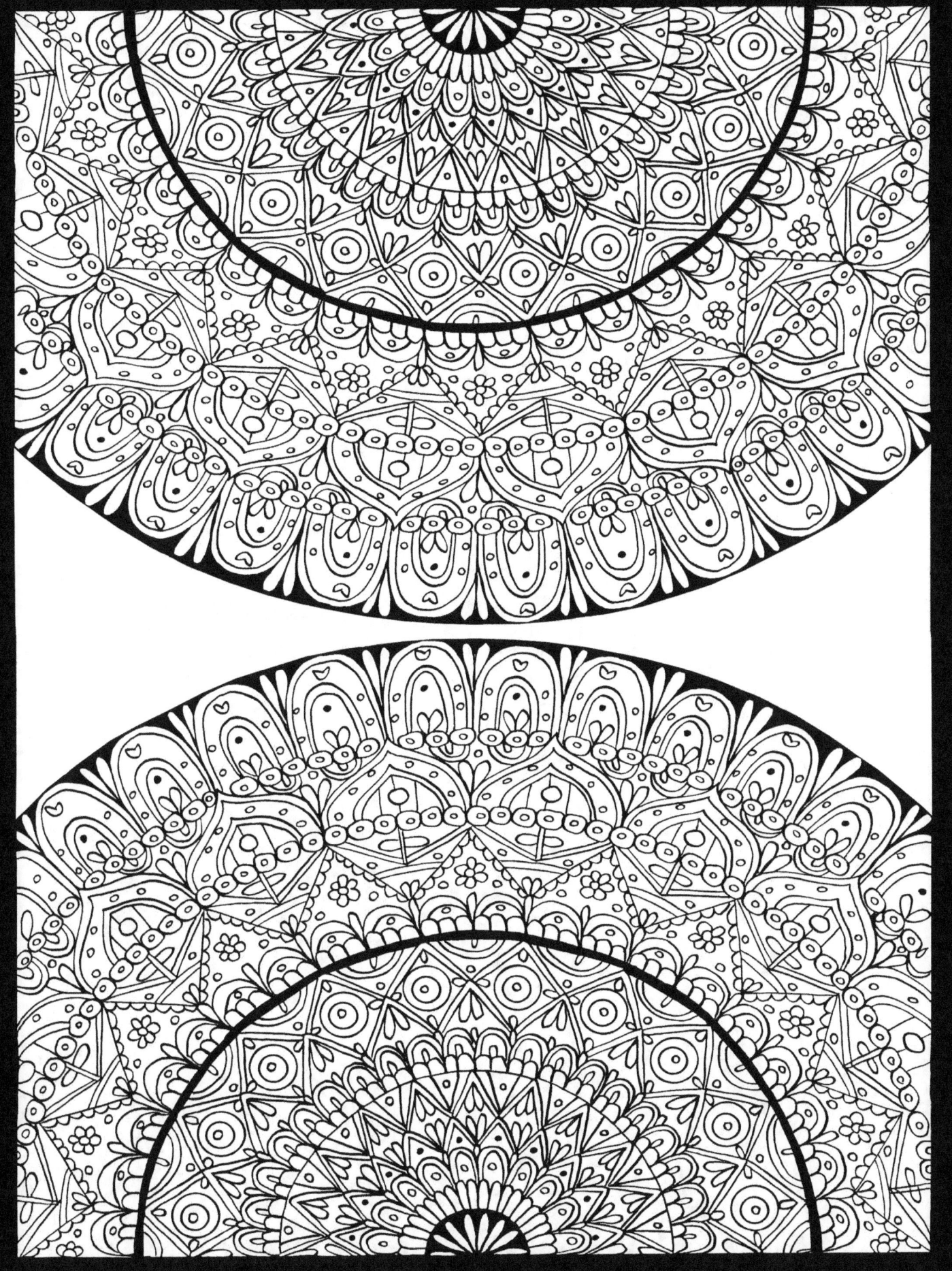

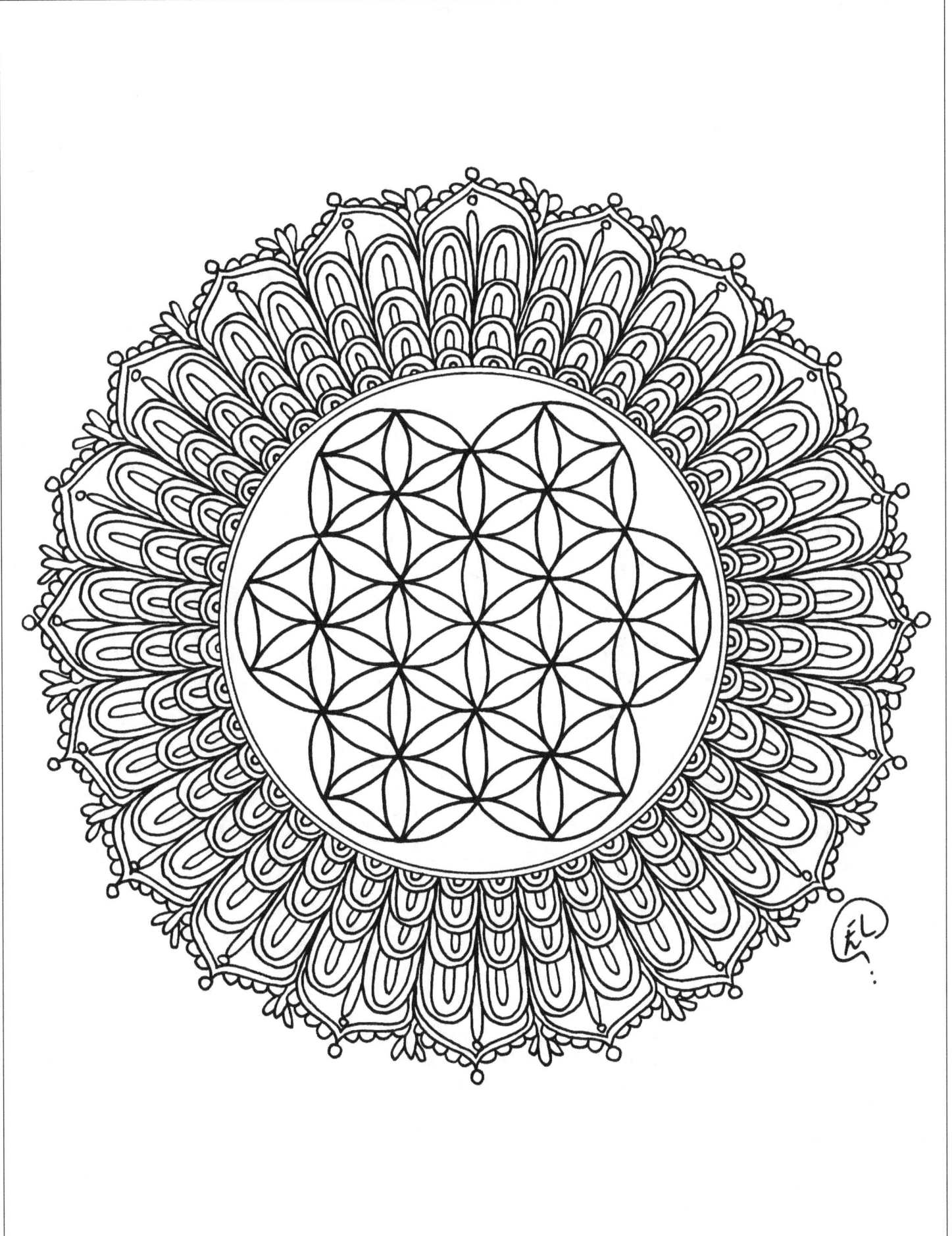

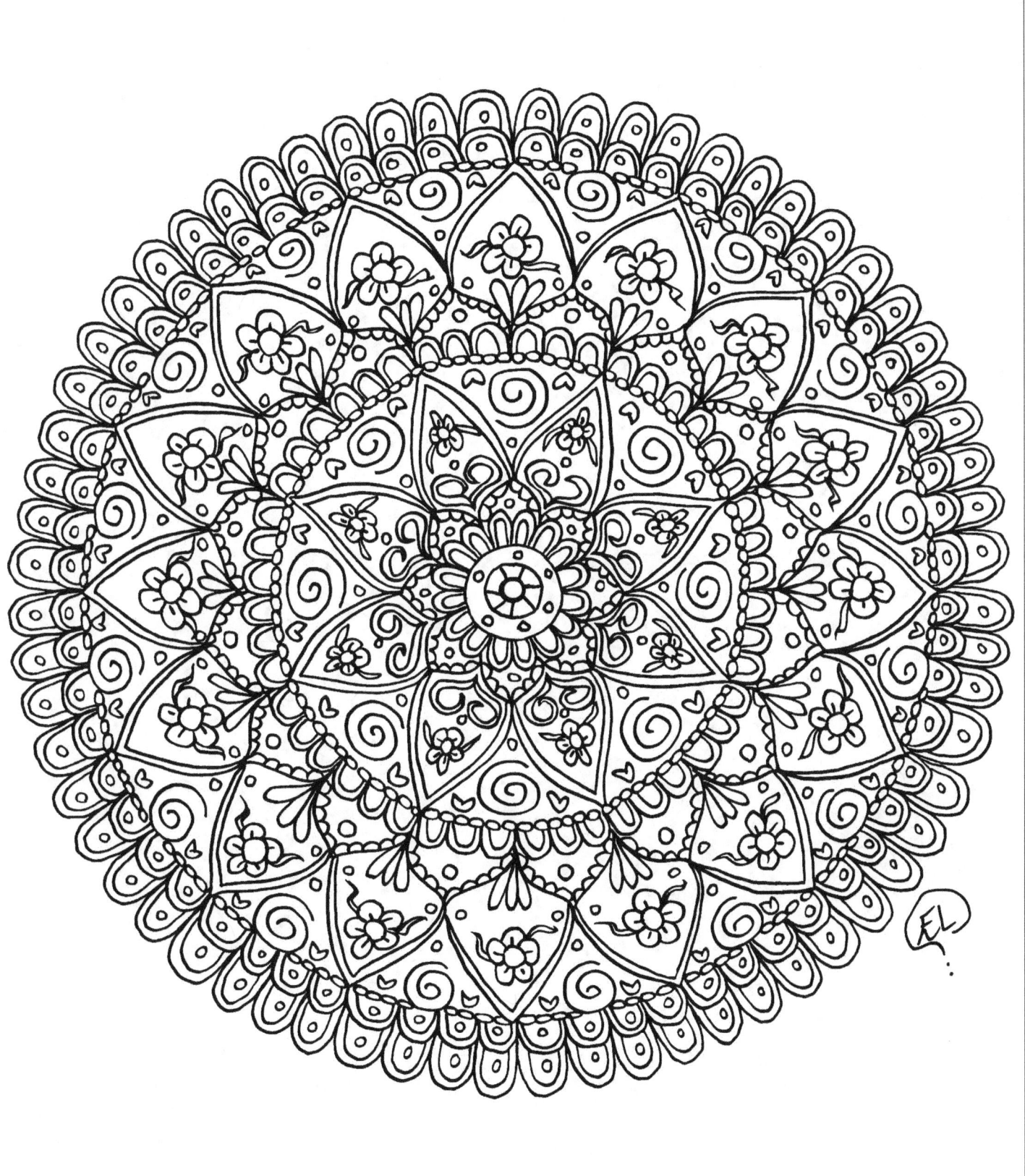

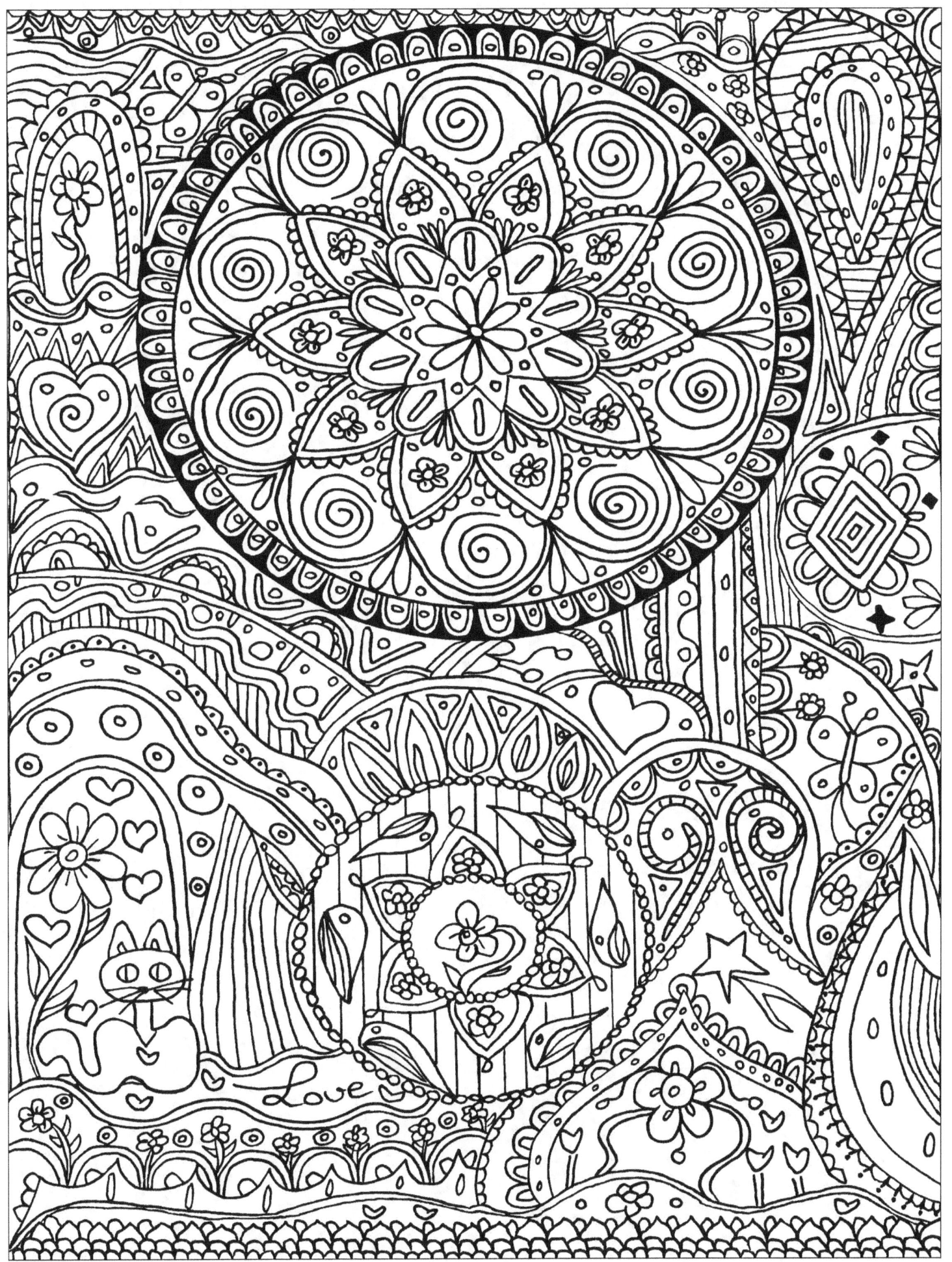

Chapter 2
Spirit of Qiw
France

Facebook : sandrine.gaucher.9

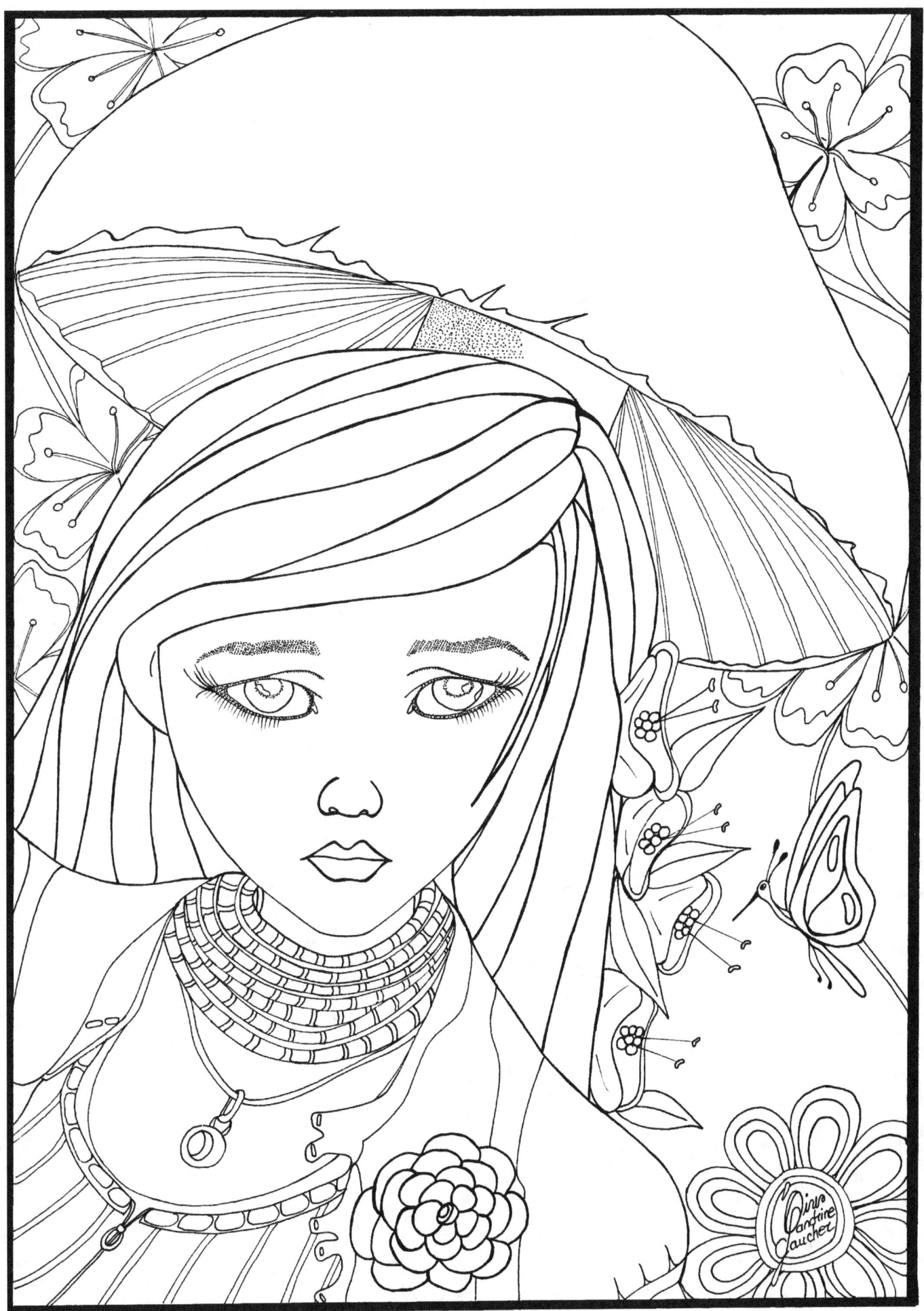

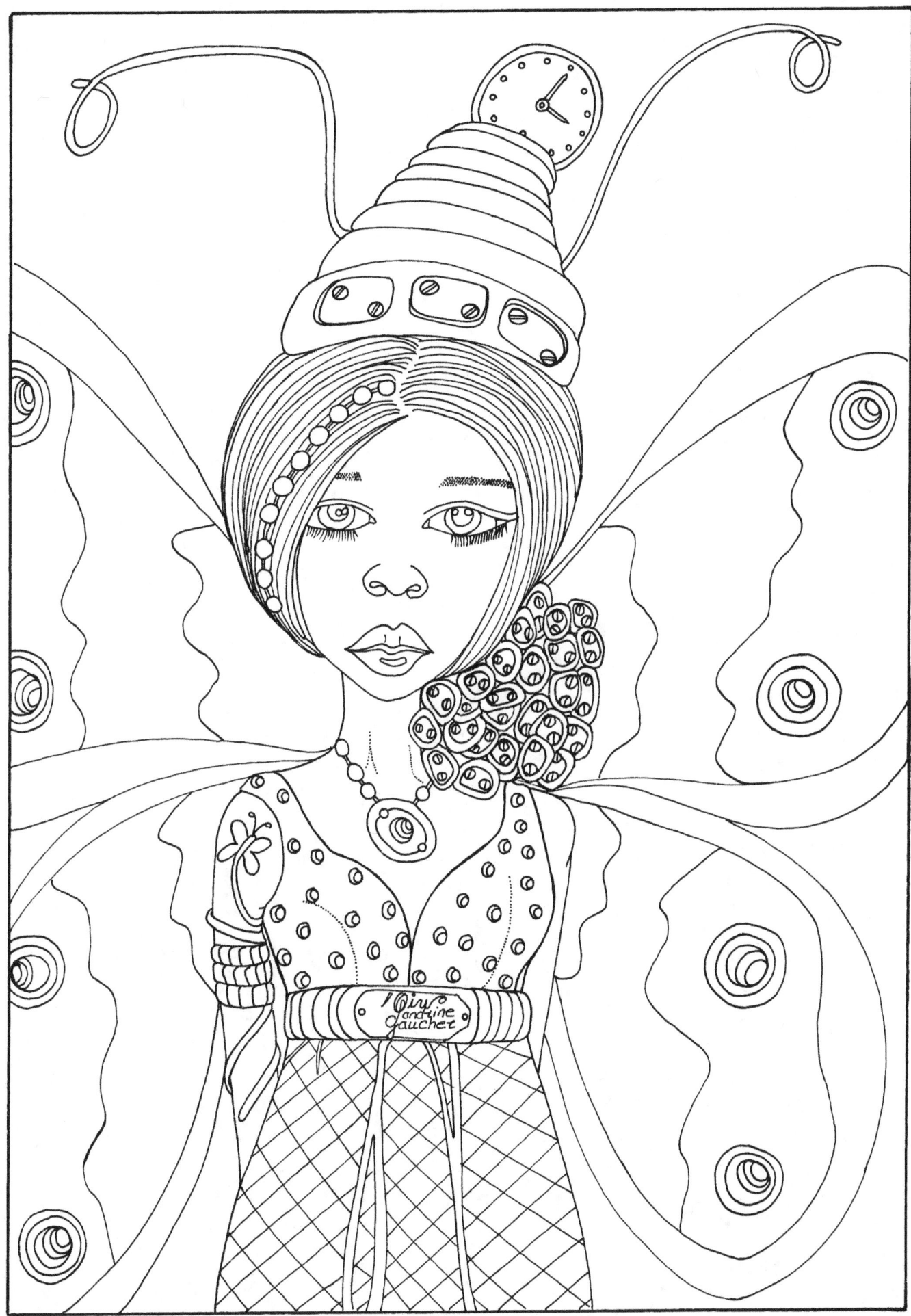

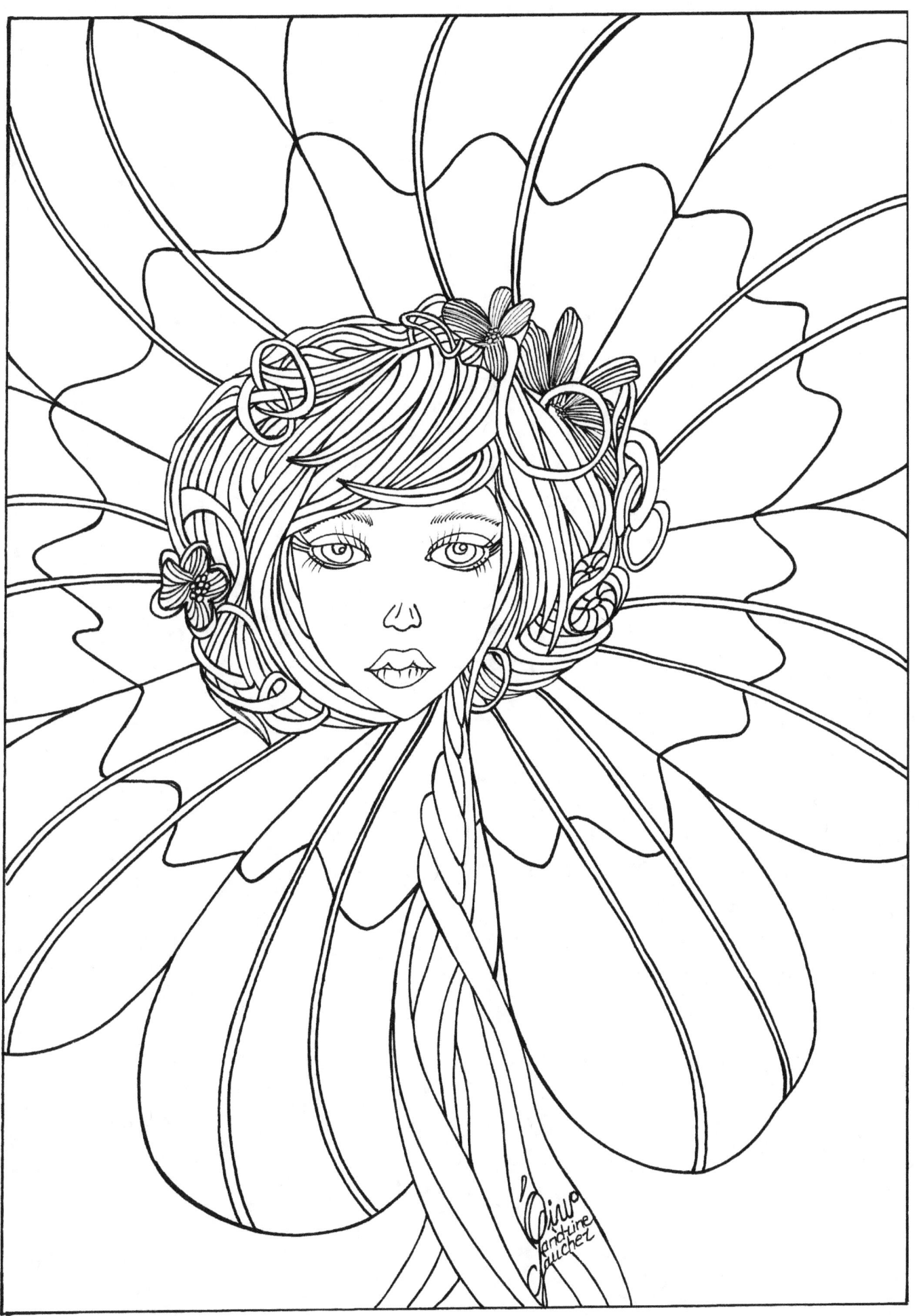

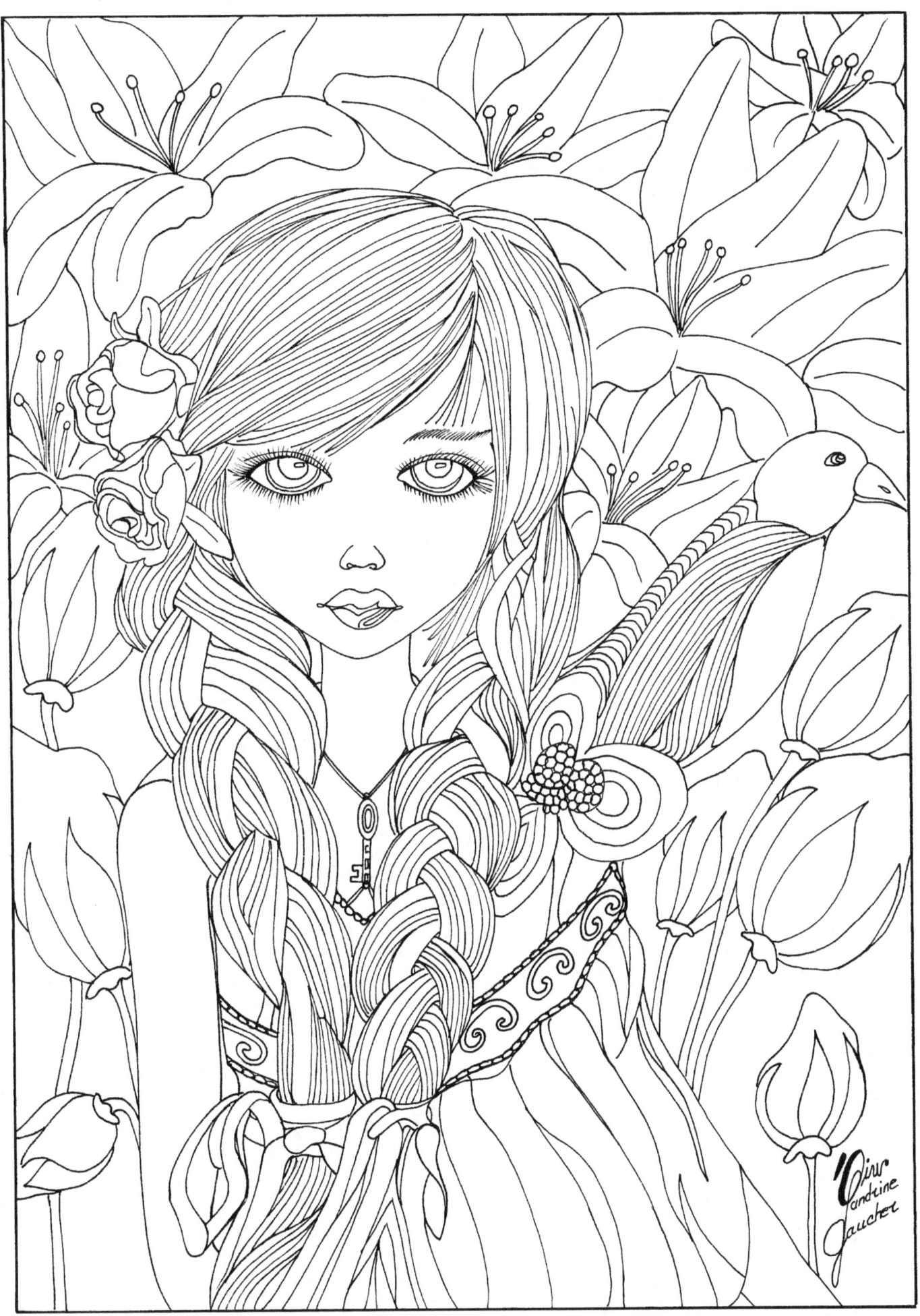

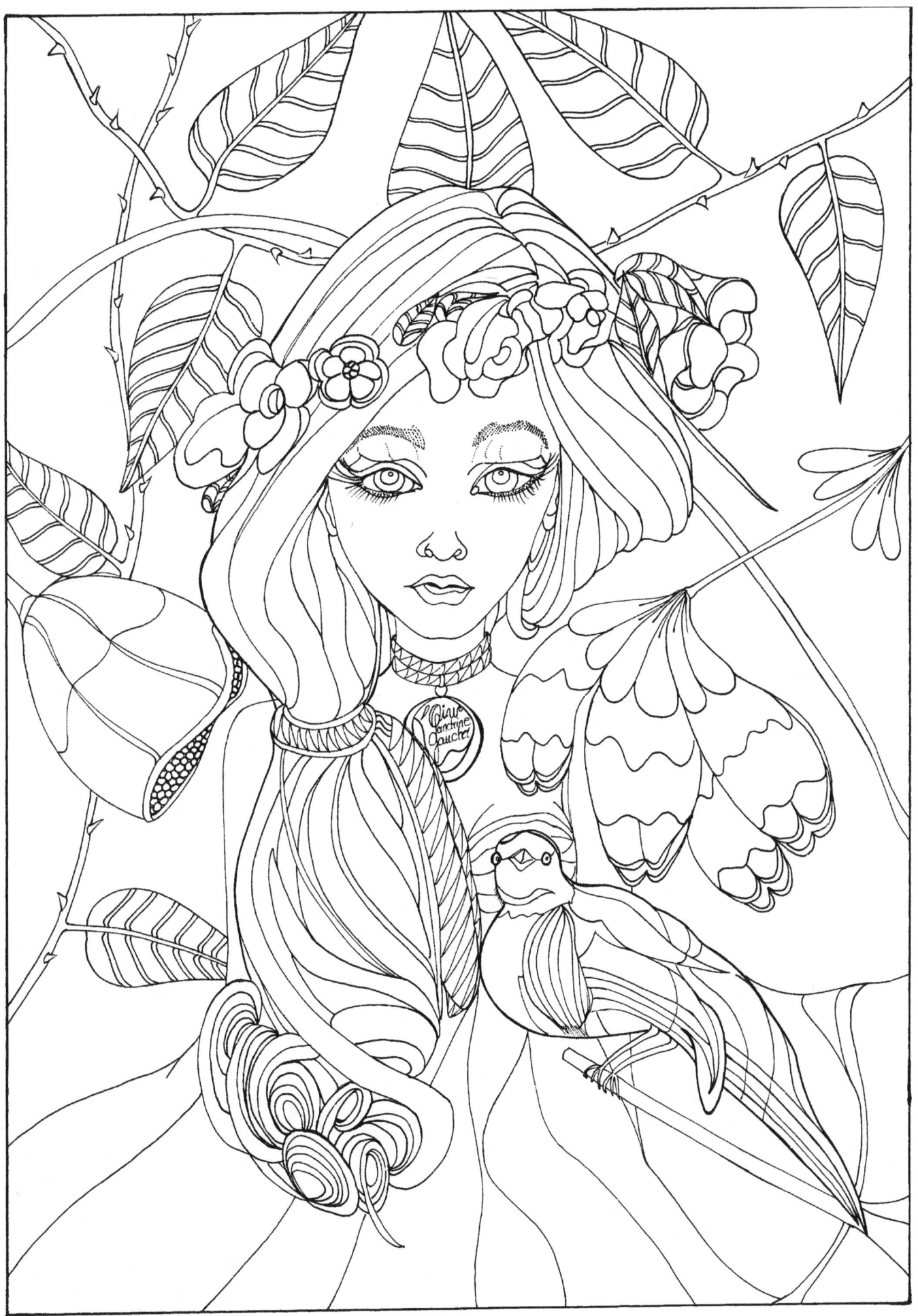

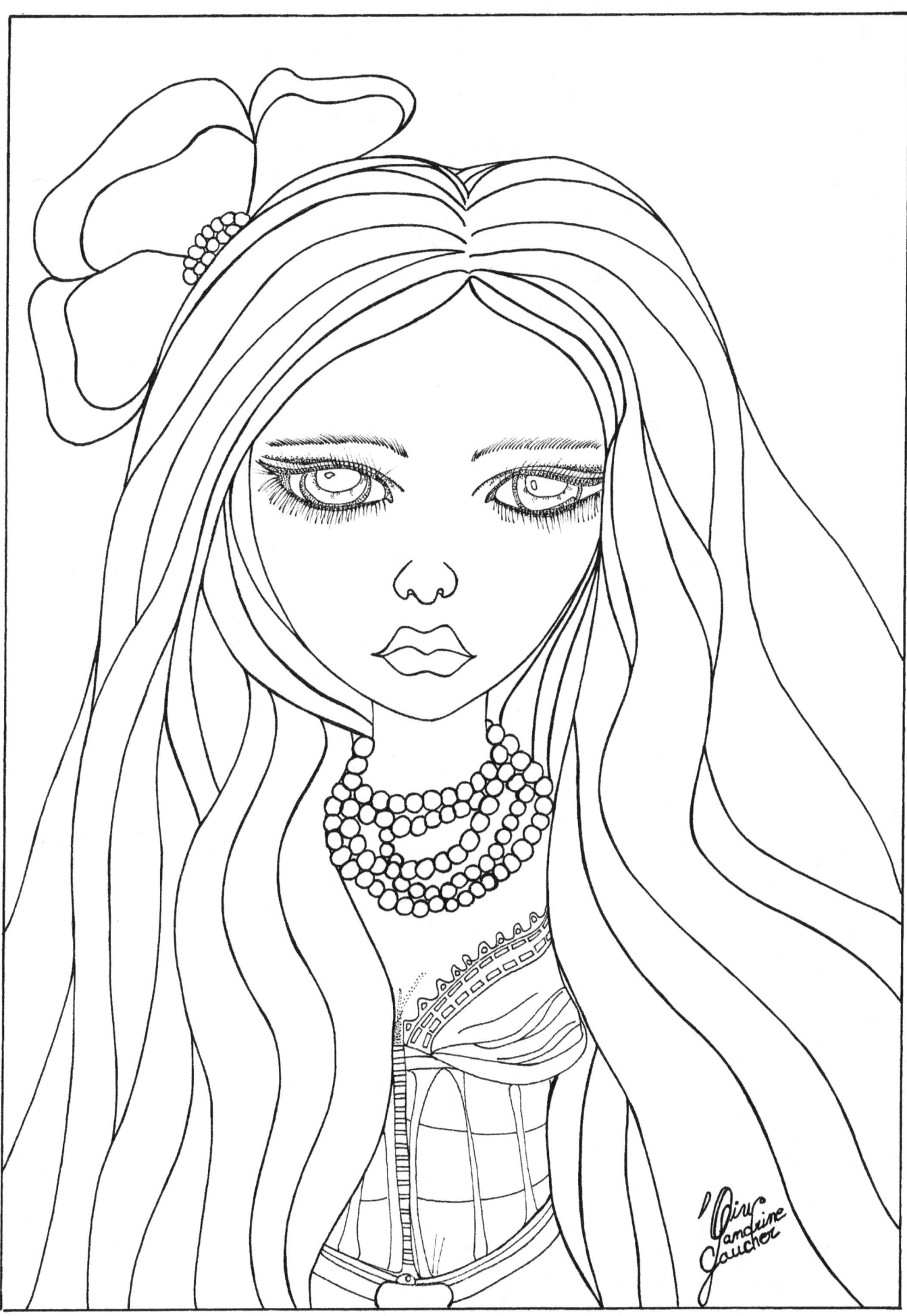

Chapter 3
Marie-Eve Klein
(mimieve)
Belgium

Facebook : "les traits'ors de mimieve"

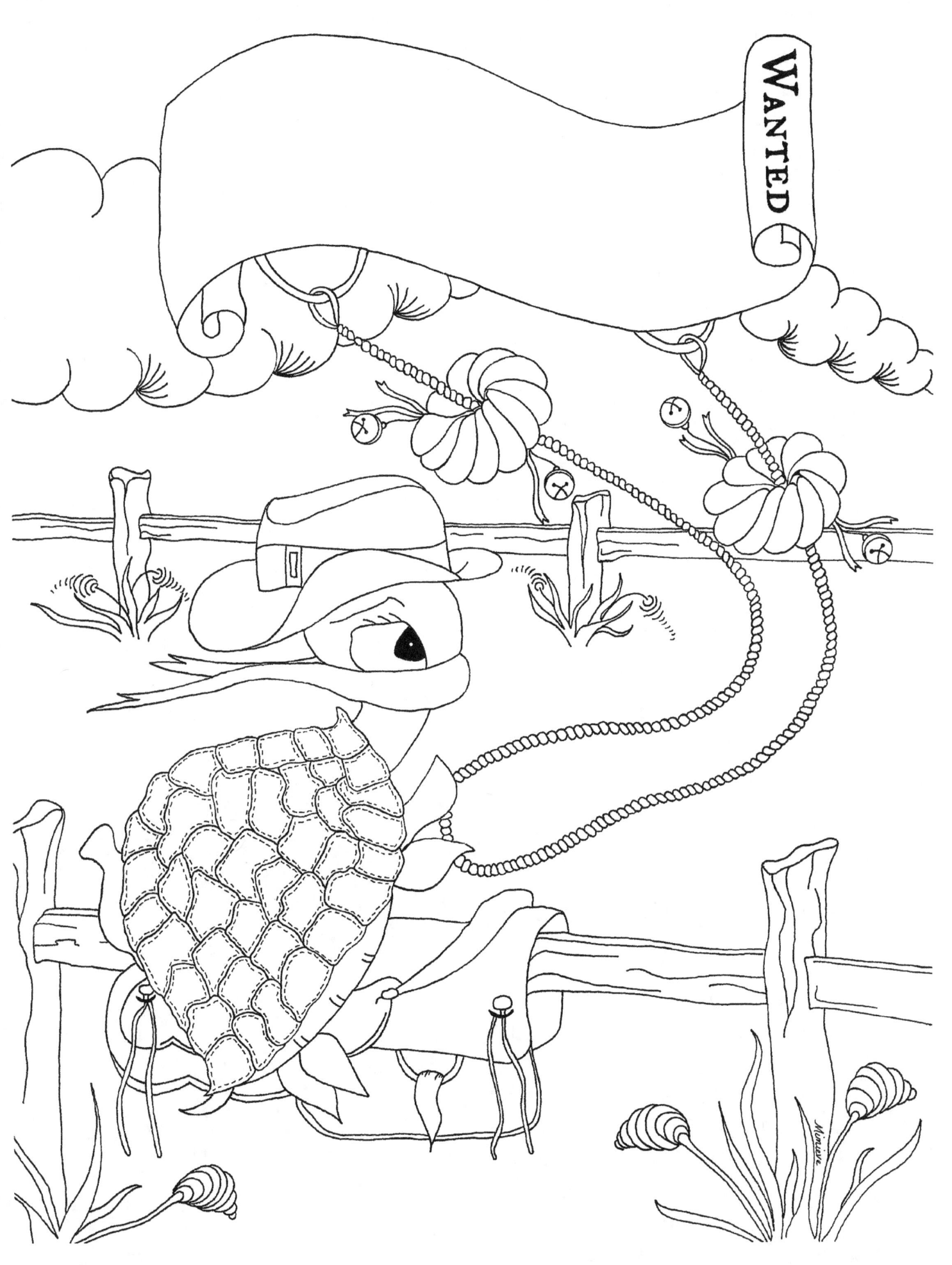

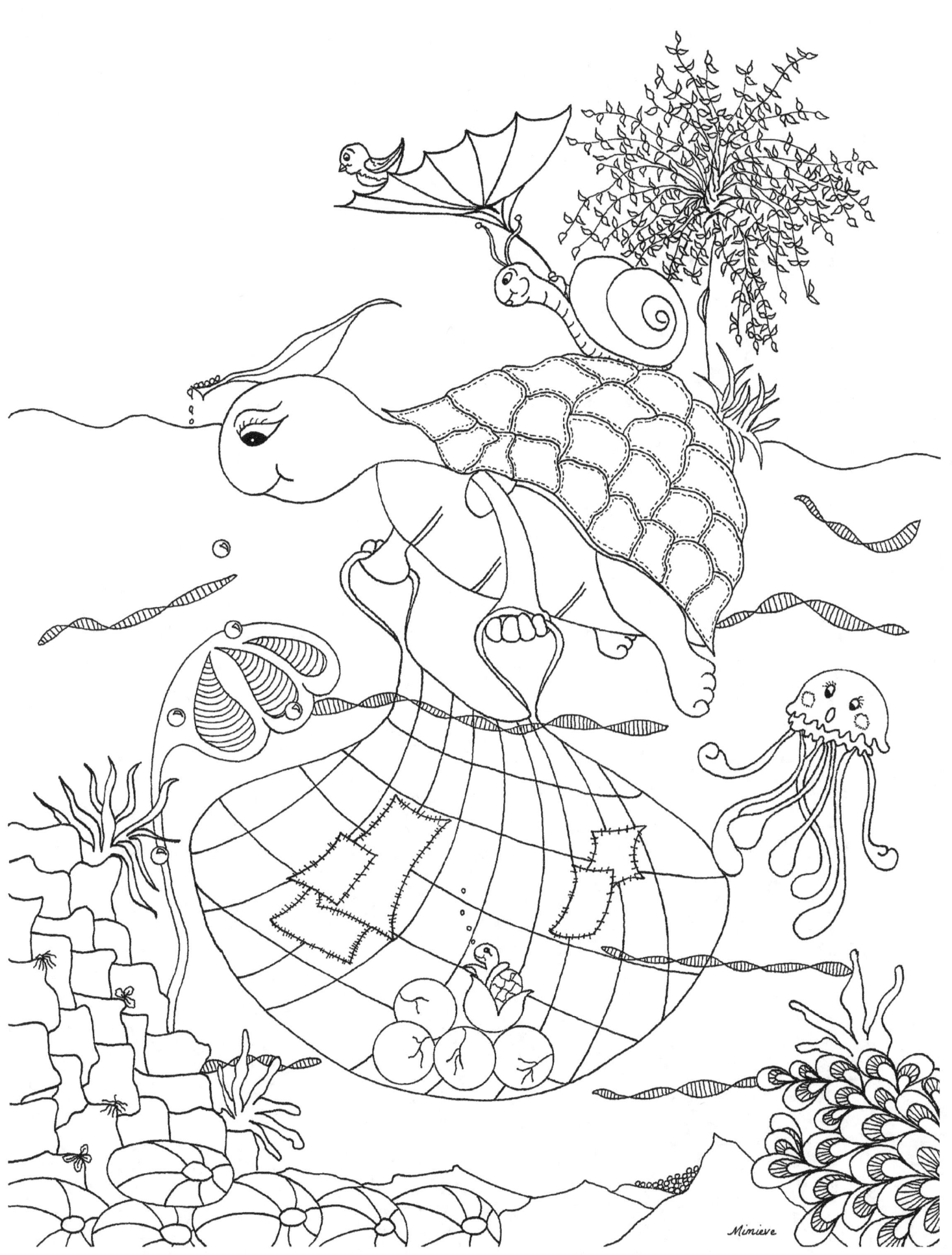

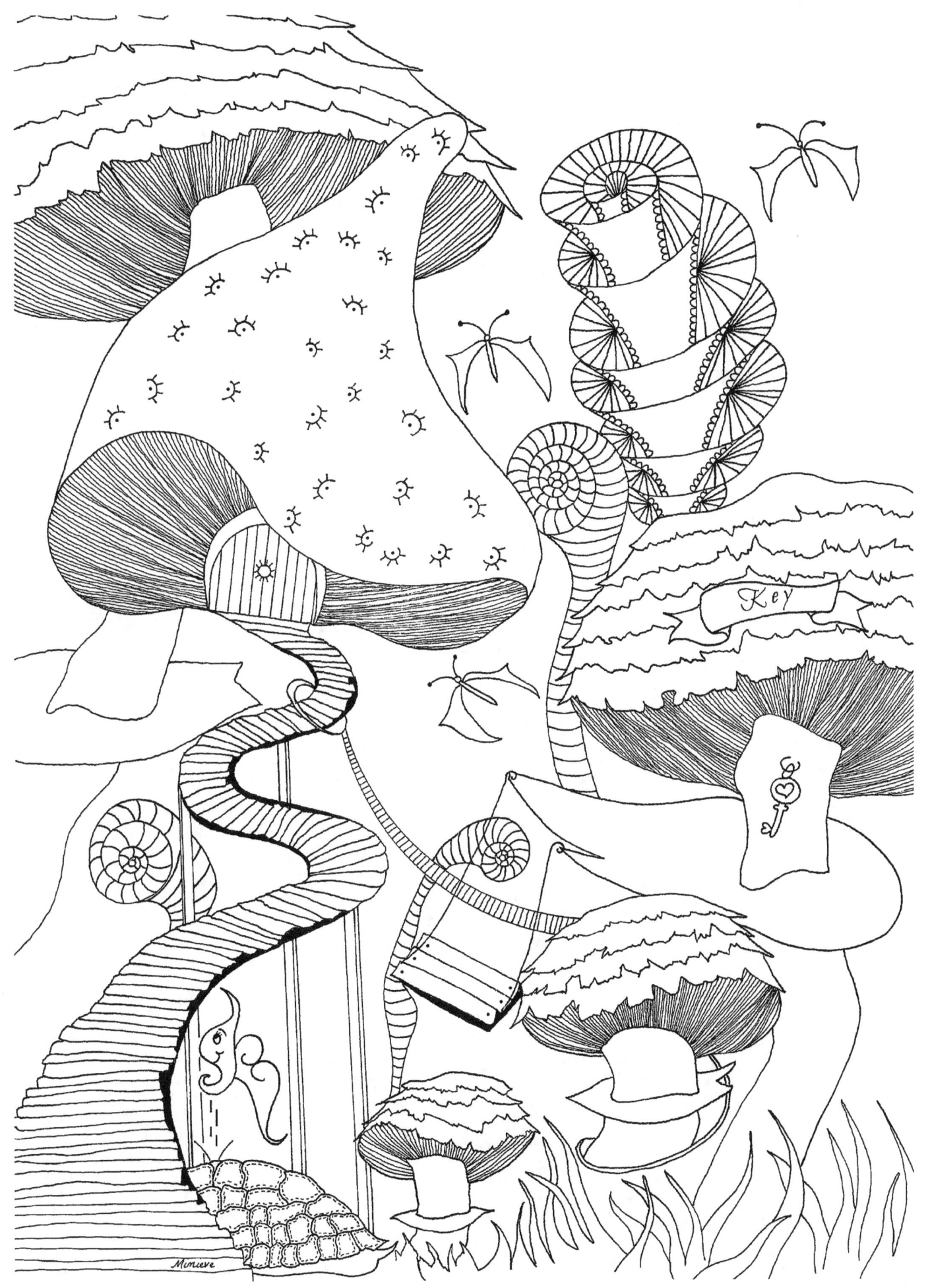

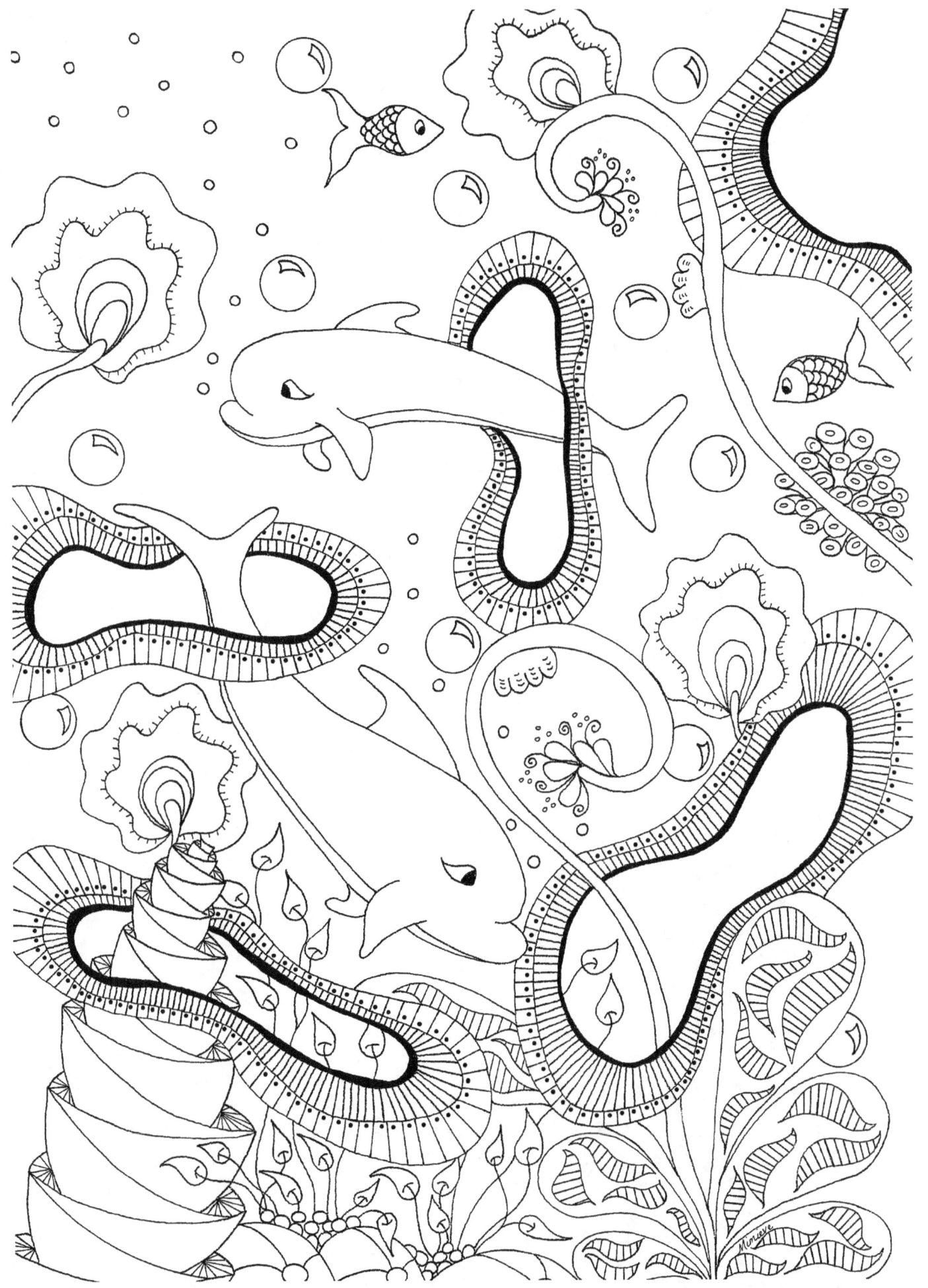

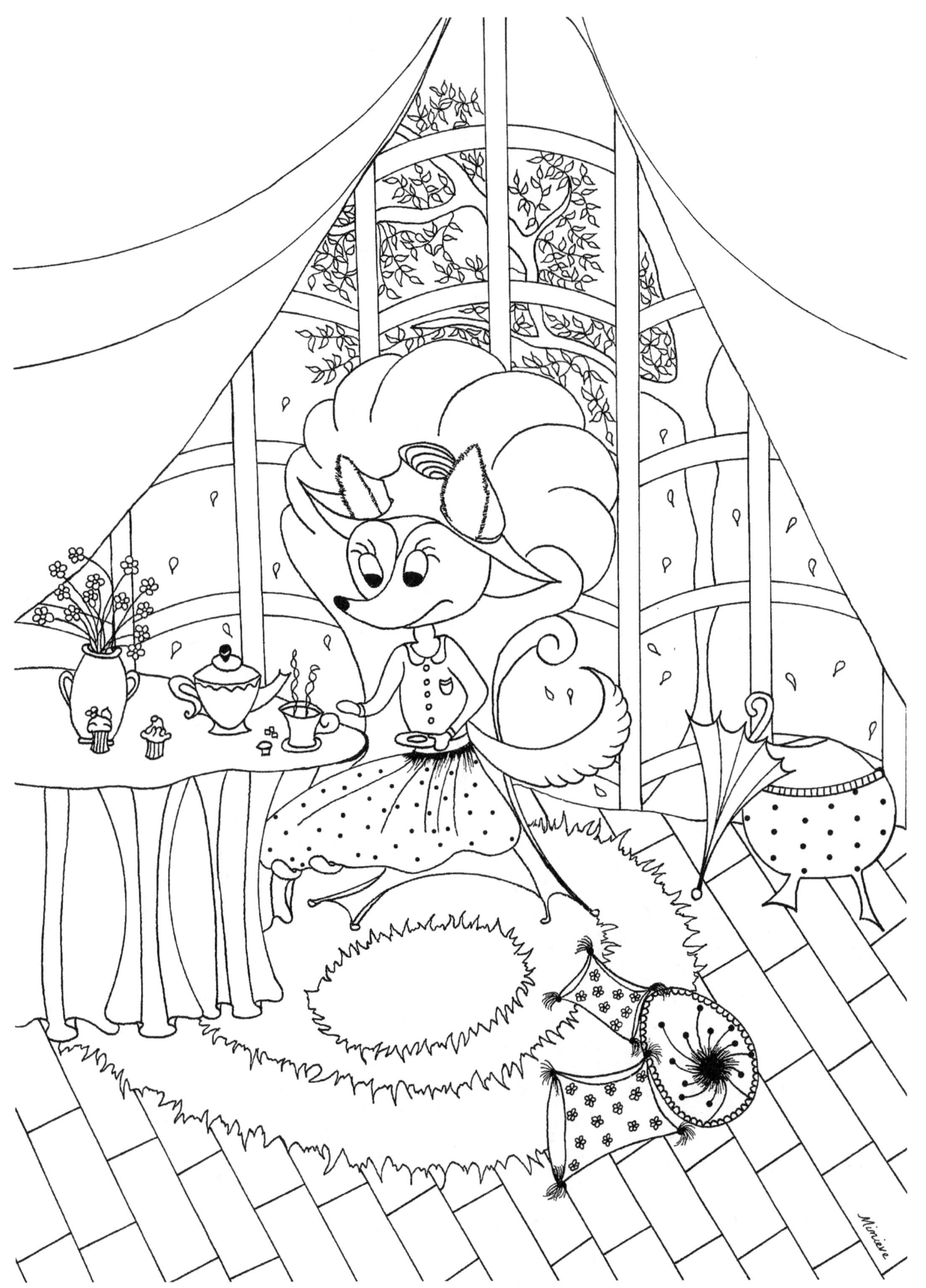

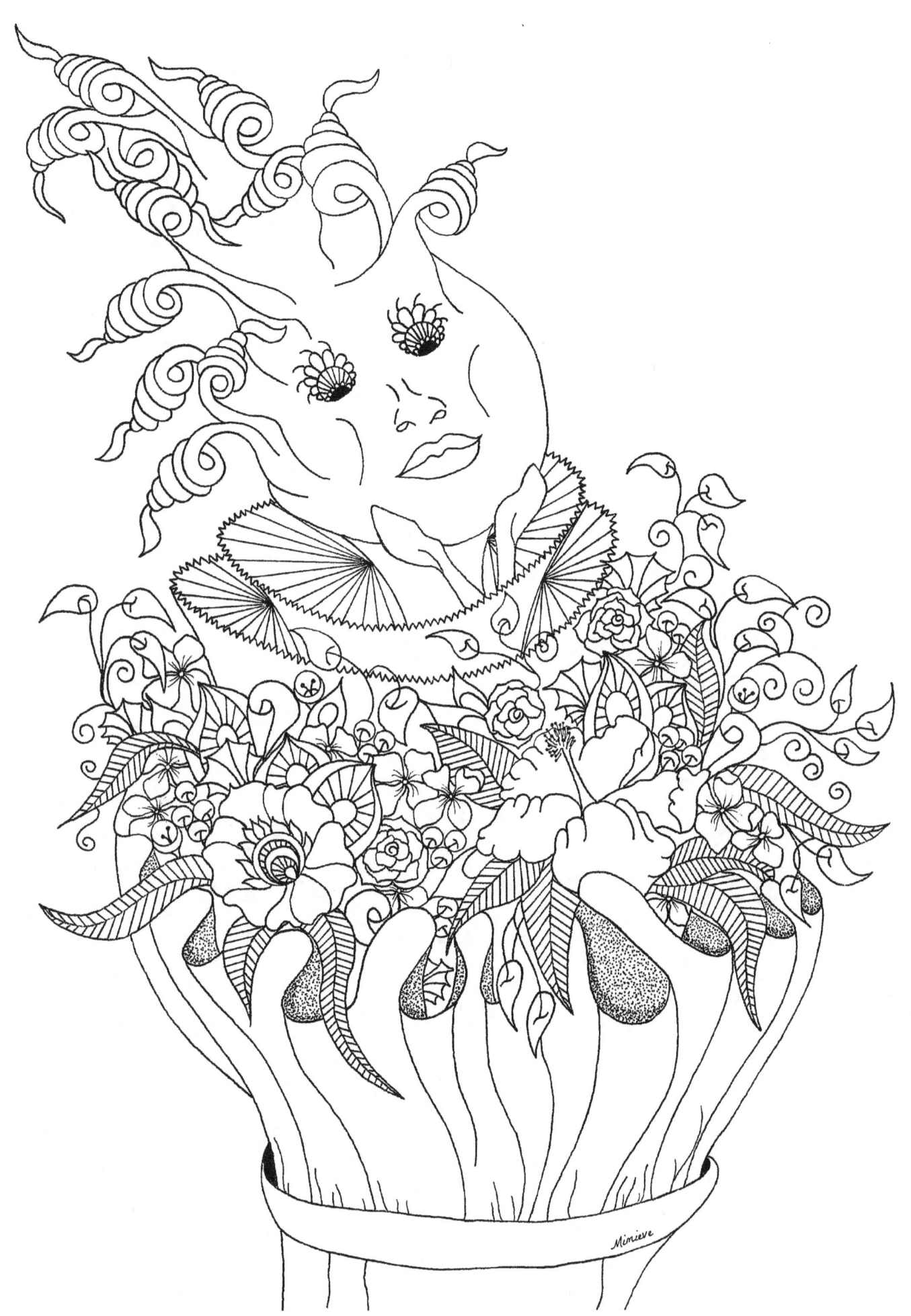

Chapter 4
Jane Levi
France

Facebook : Cheeky-CatsJane-Levi-

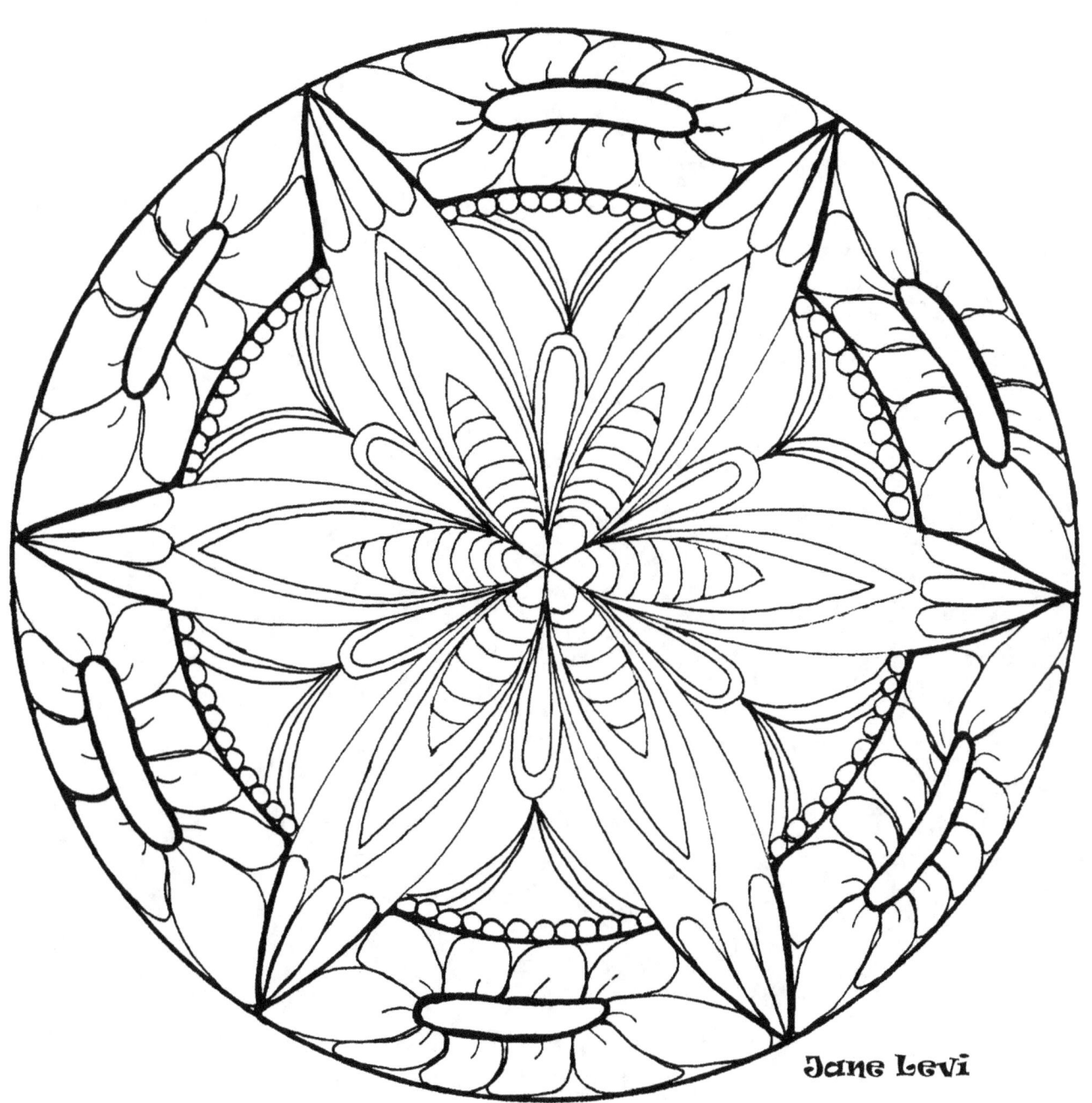

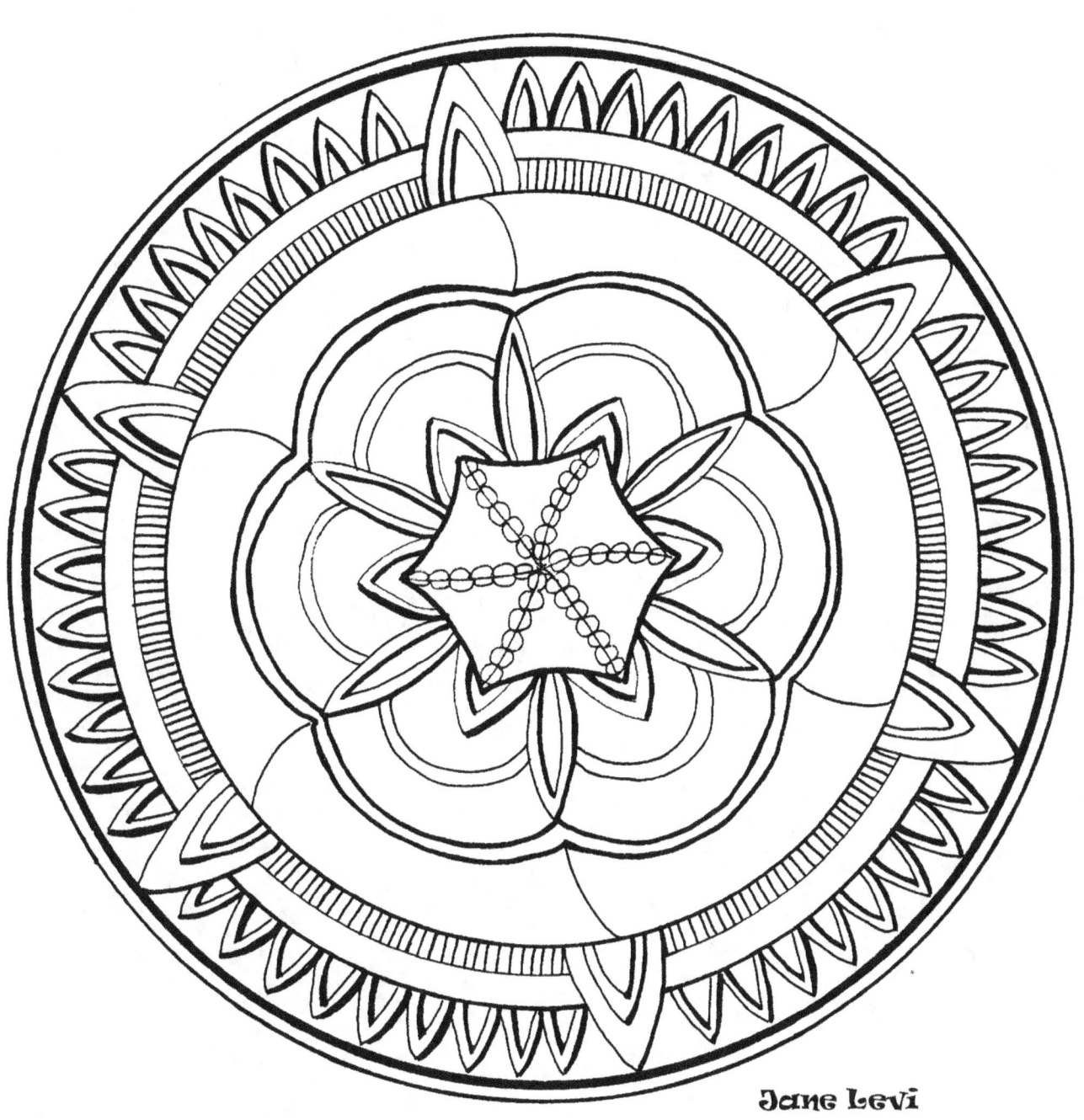

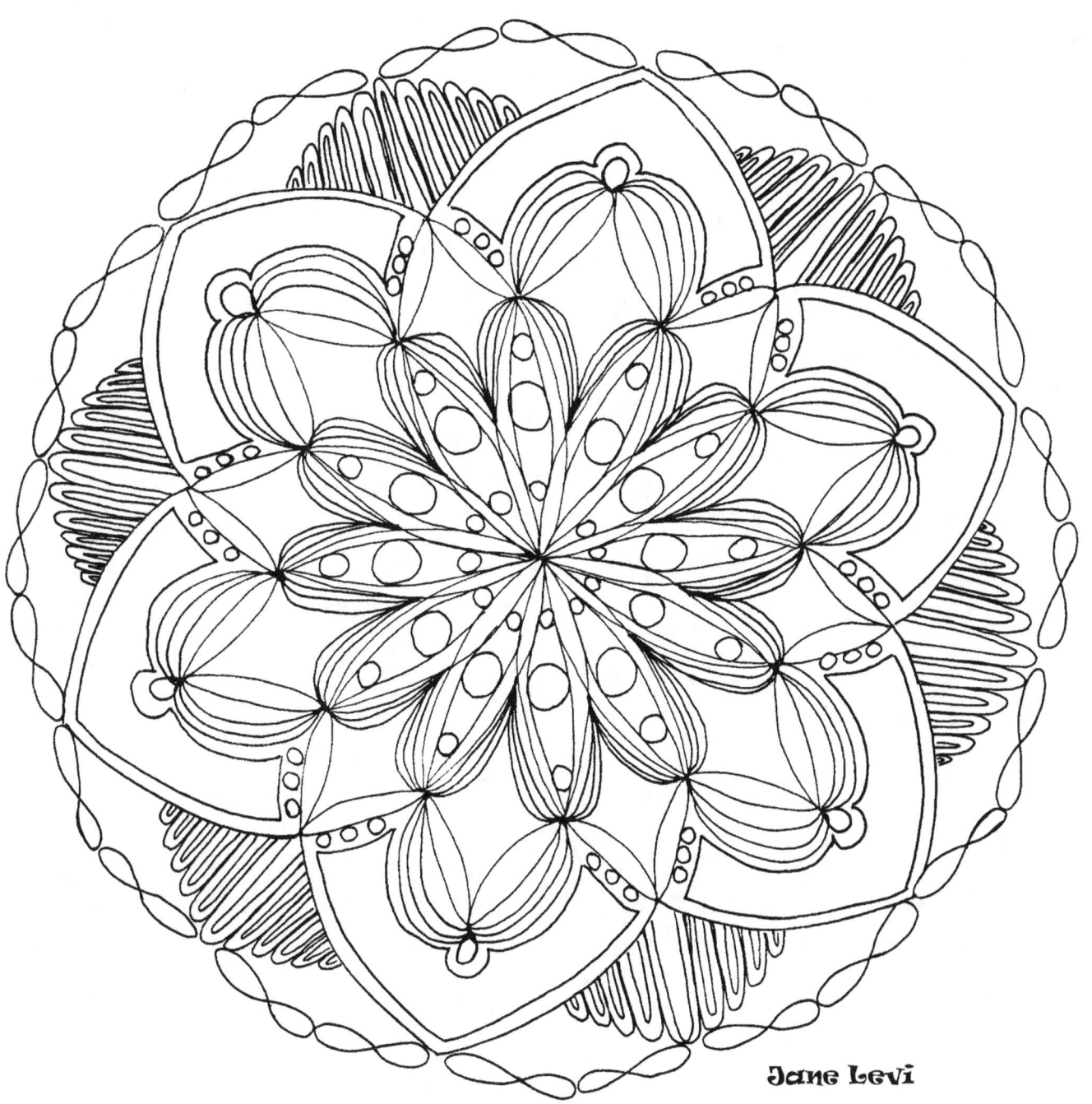

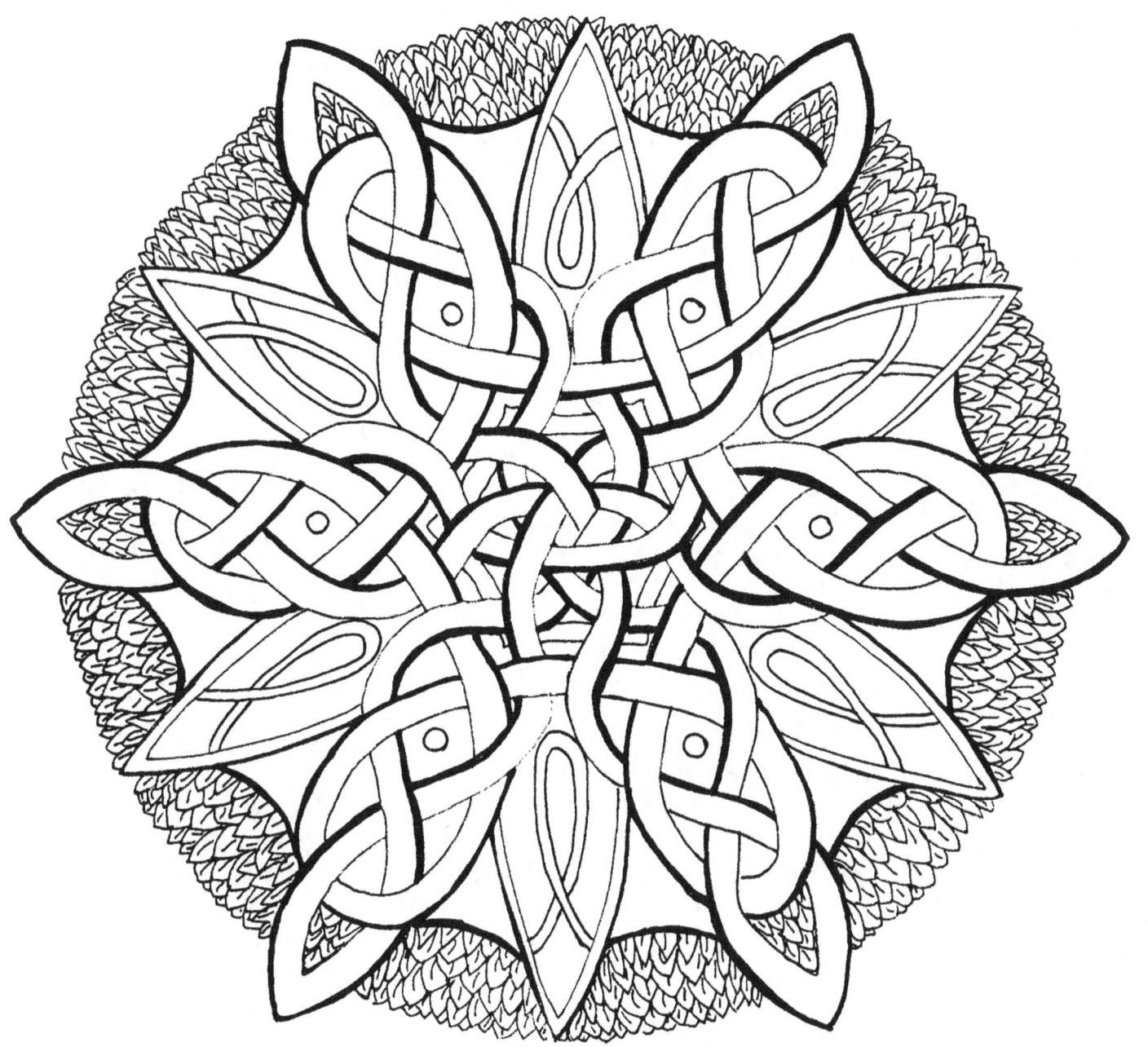

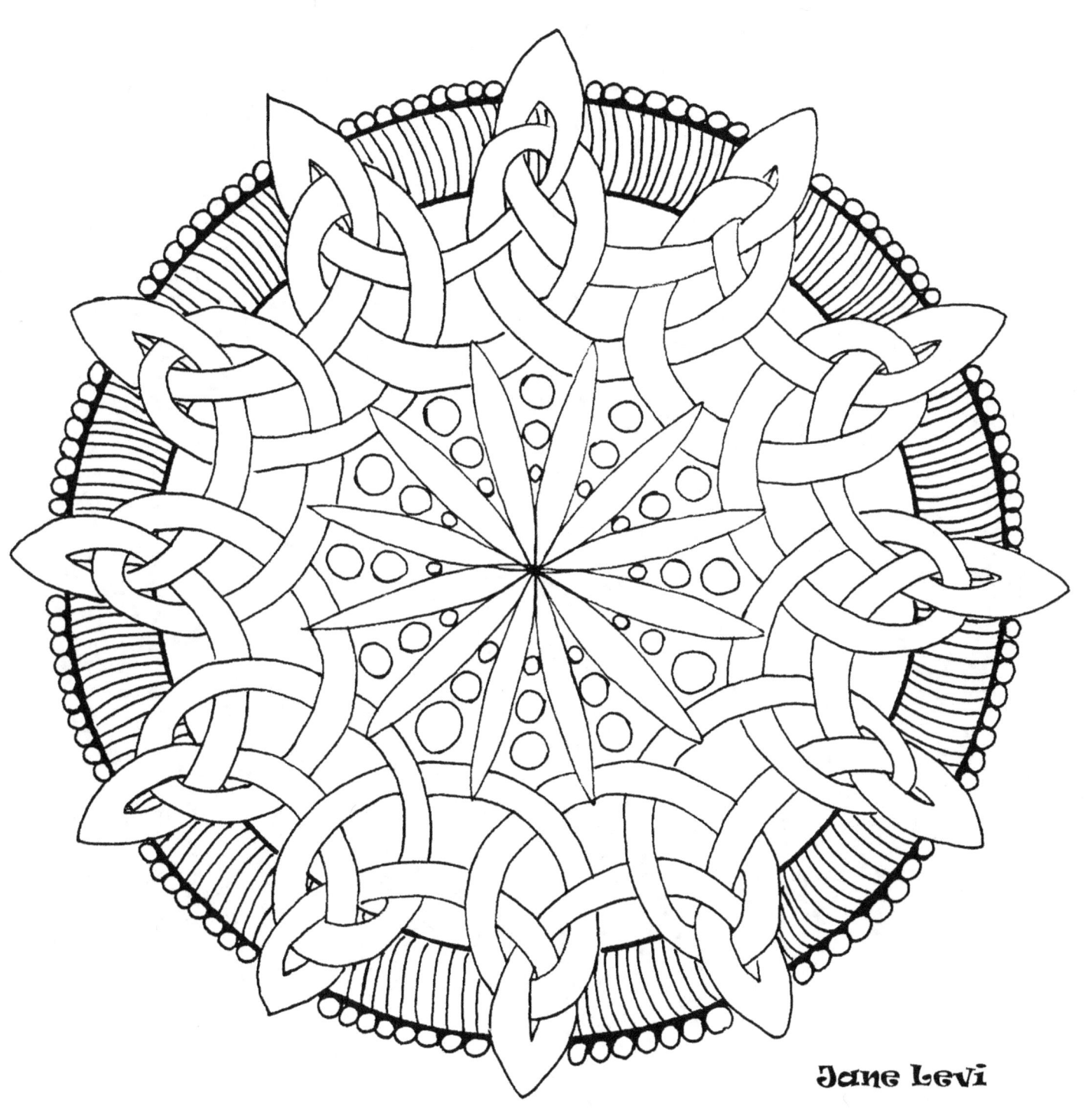

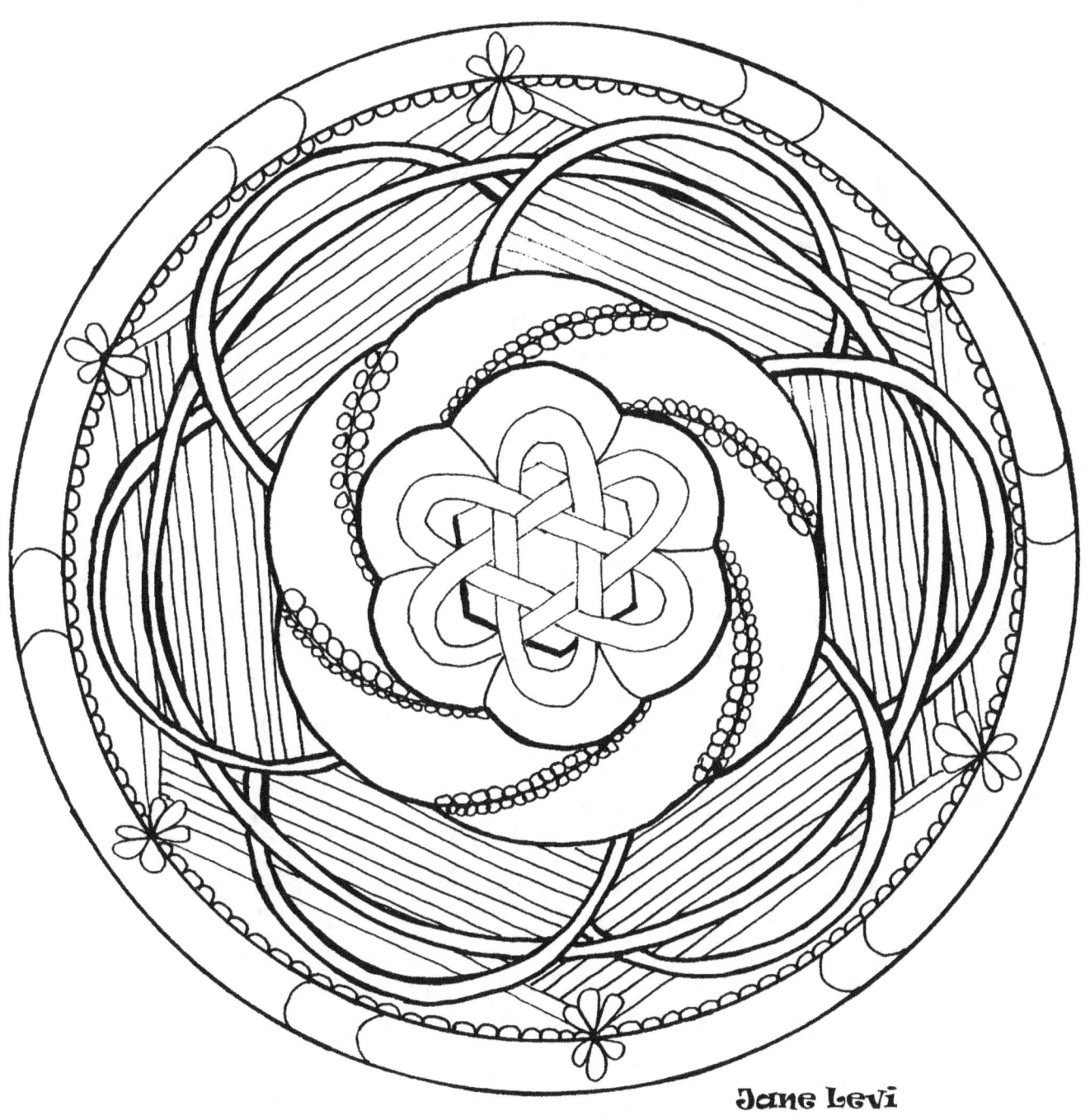

Chapter 5
Irina Sergeeva
Russia

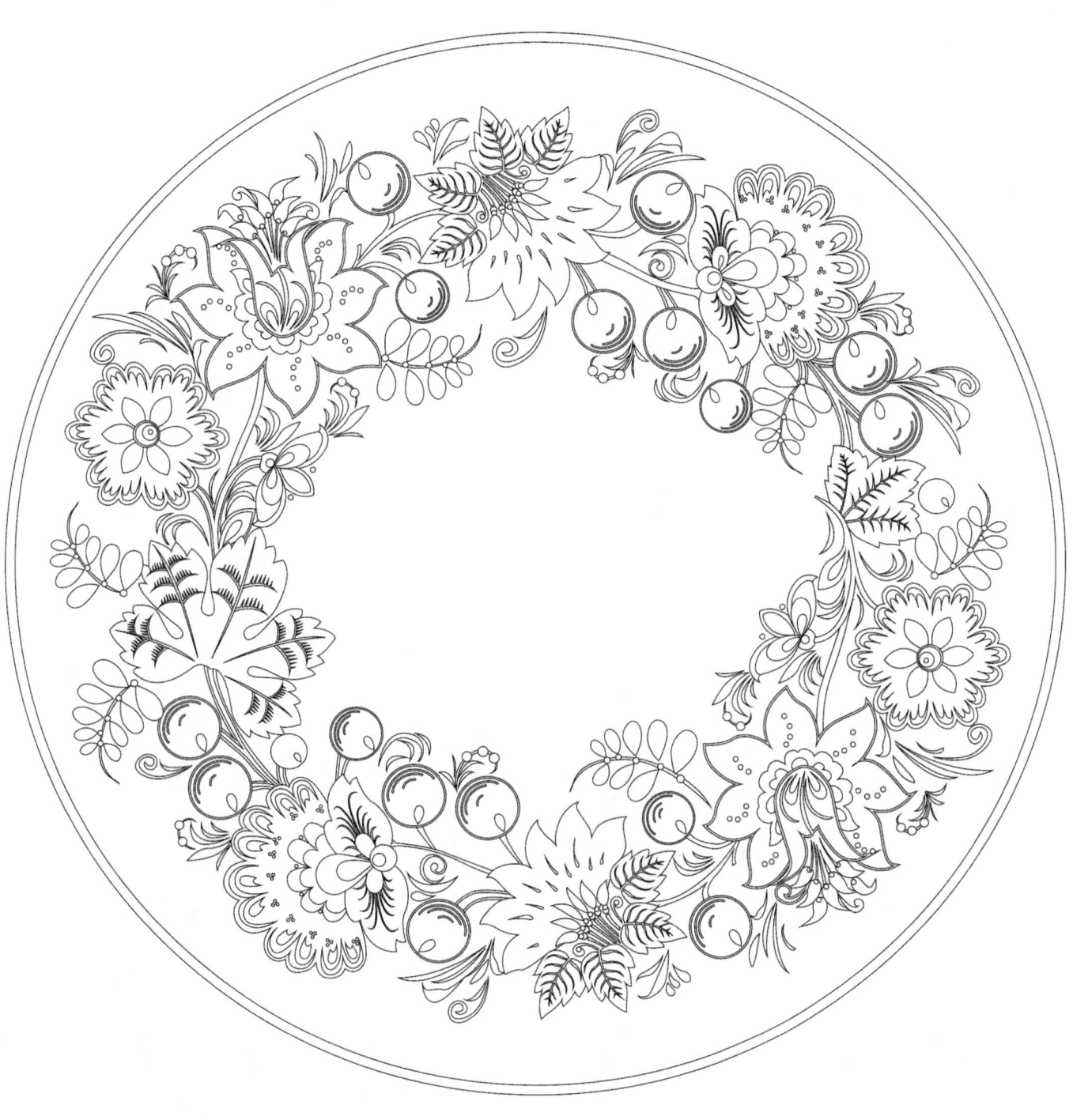

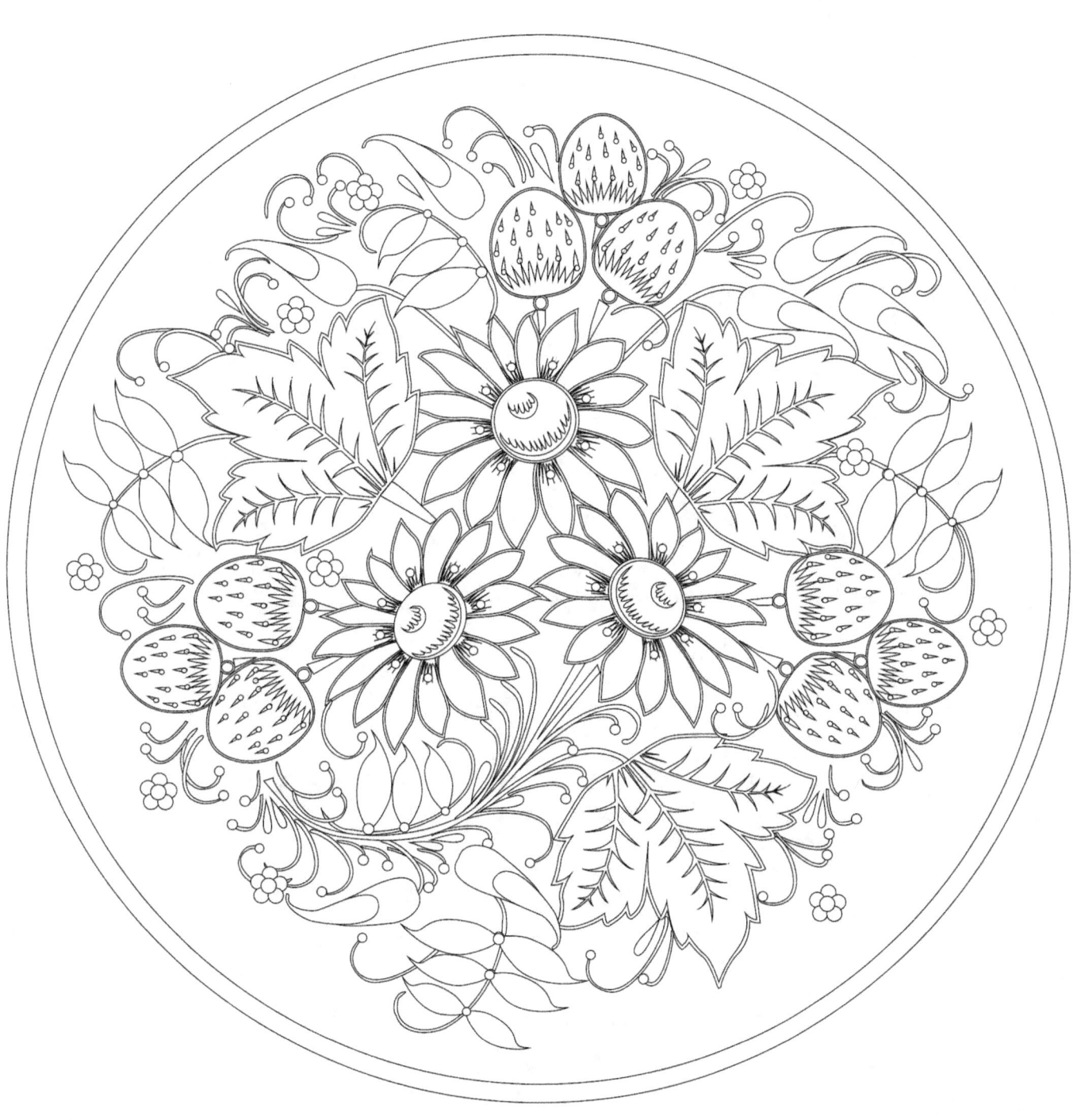

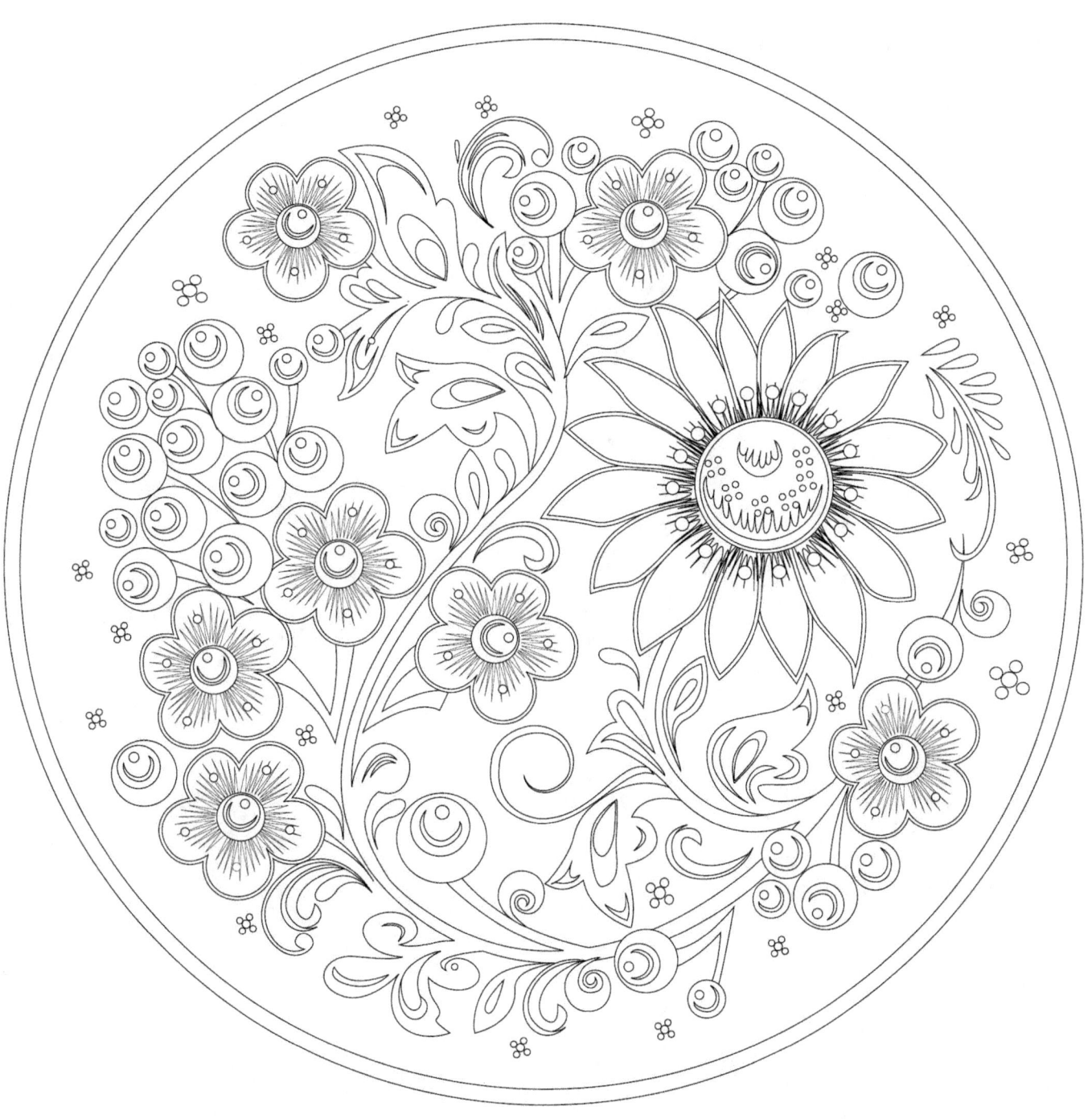

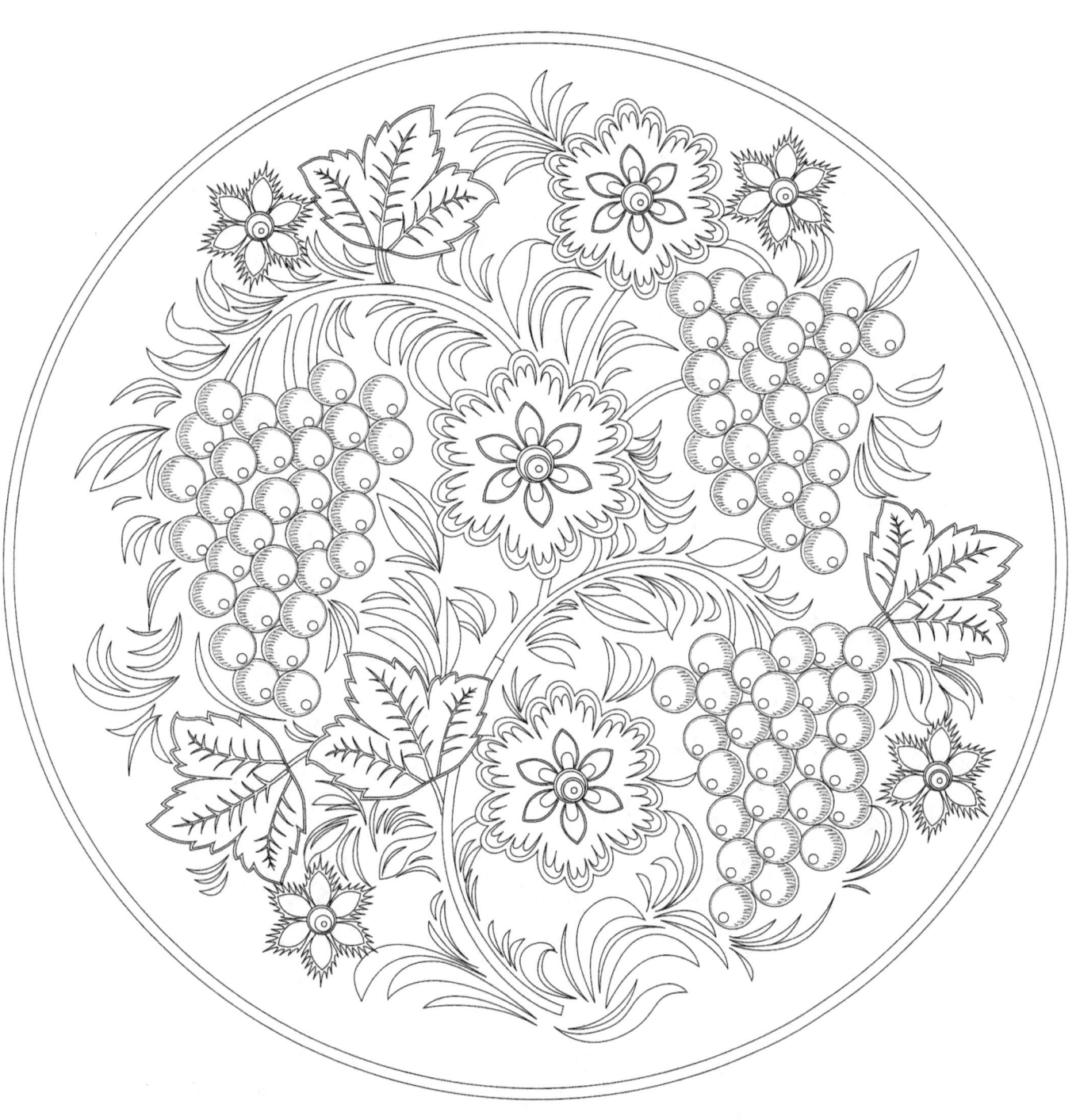

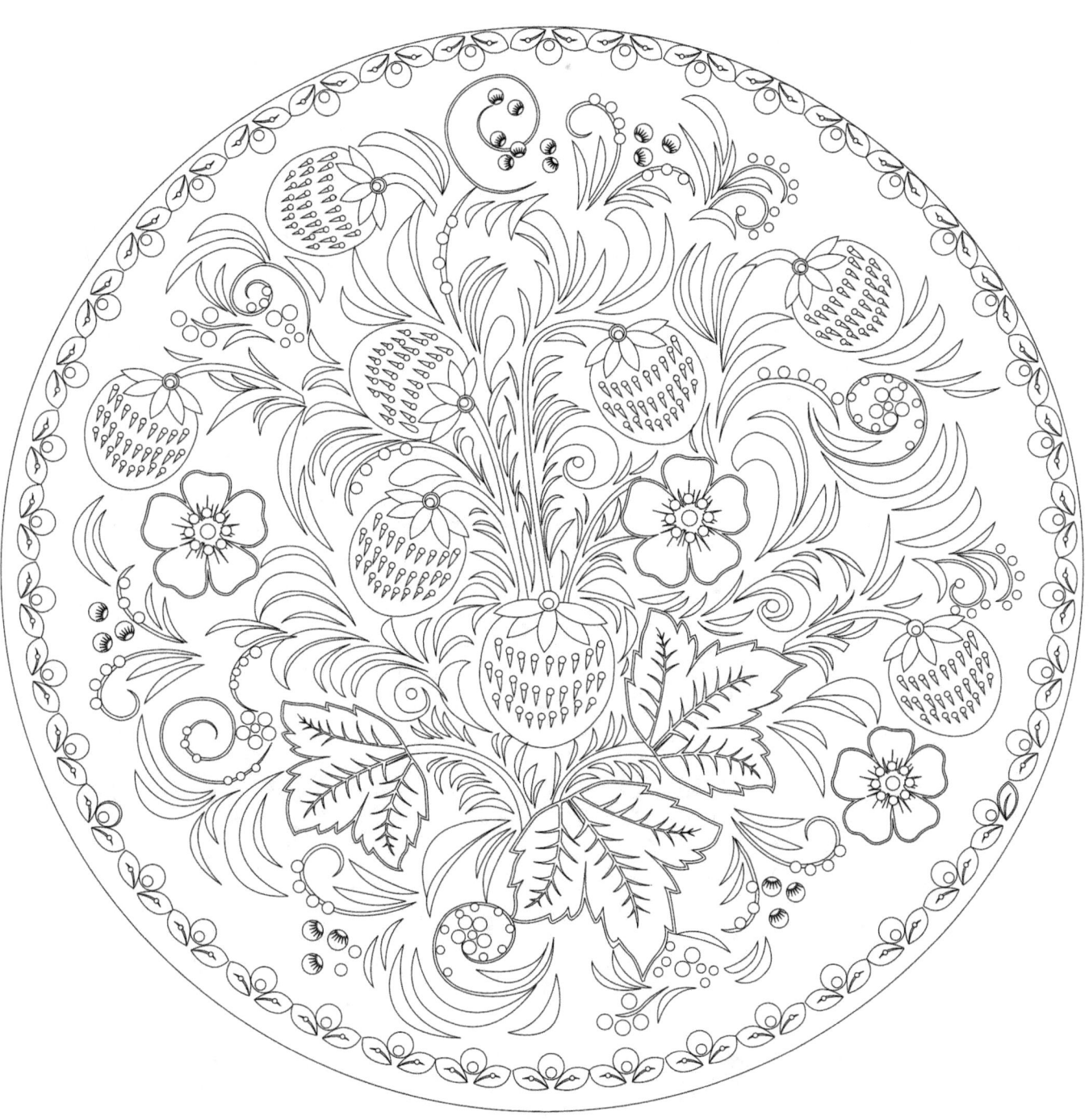

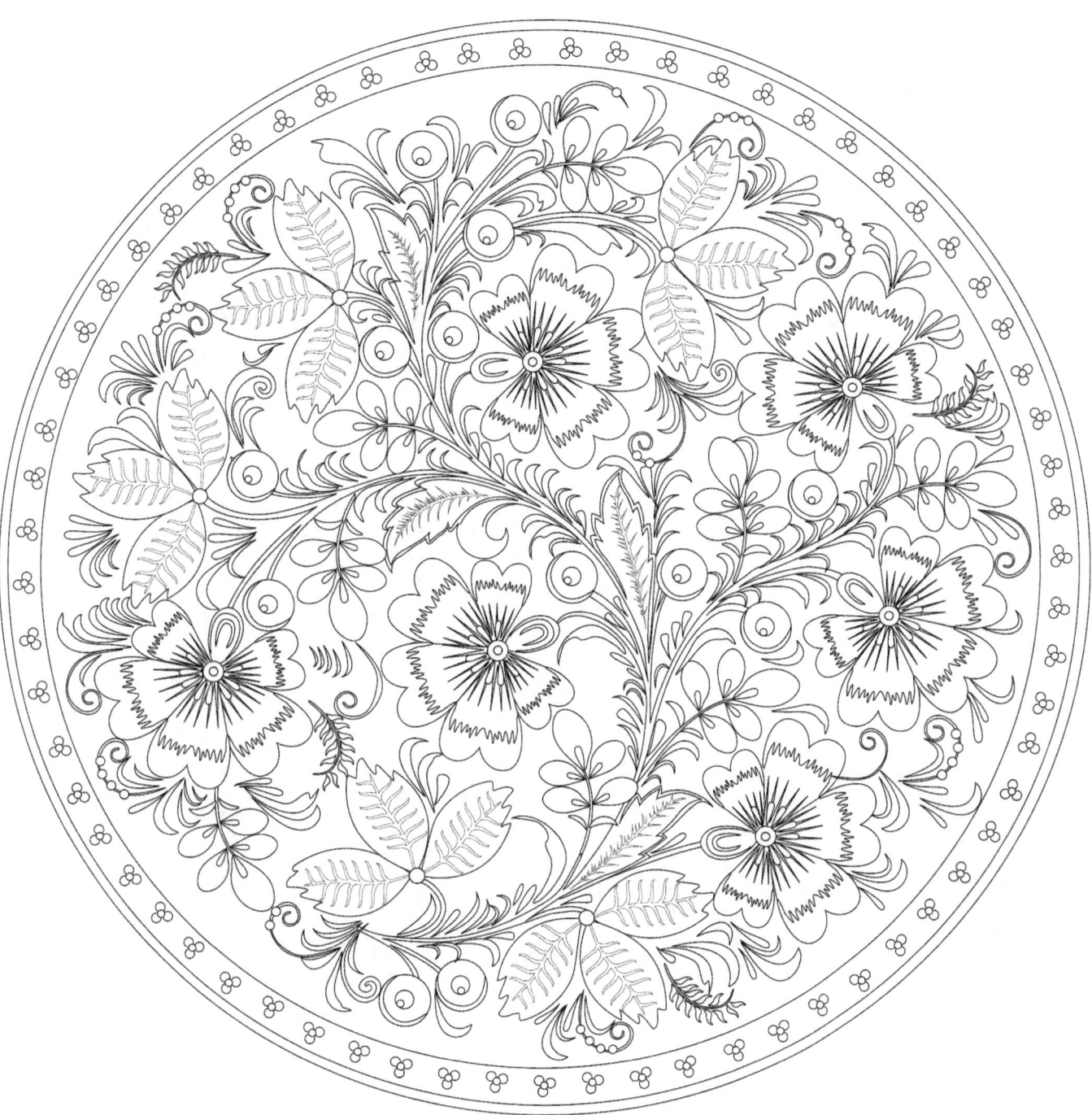

Chapter 6
Joann Sands
United Kingdom

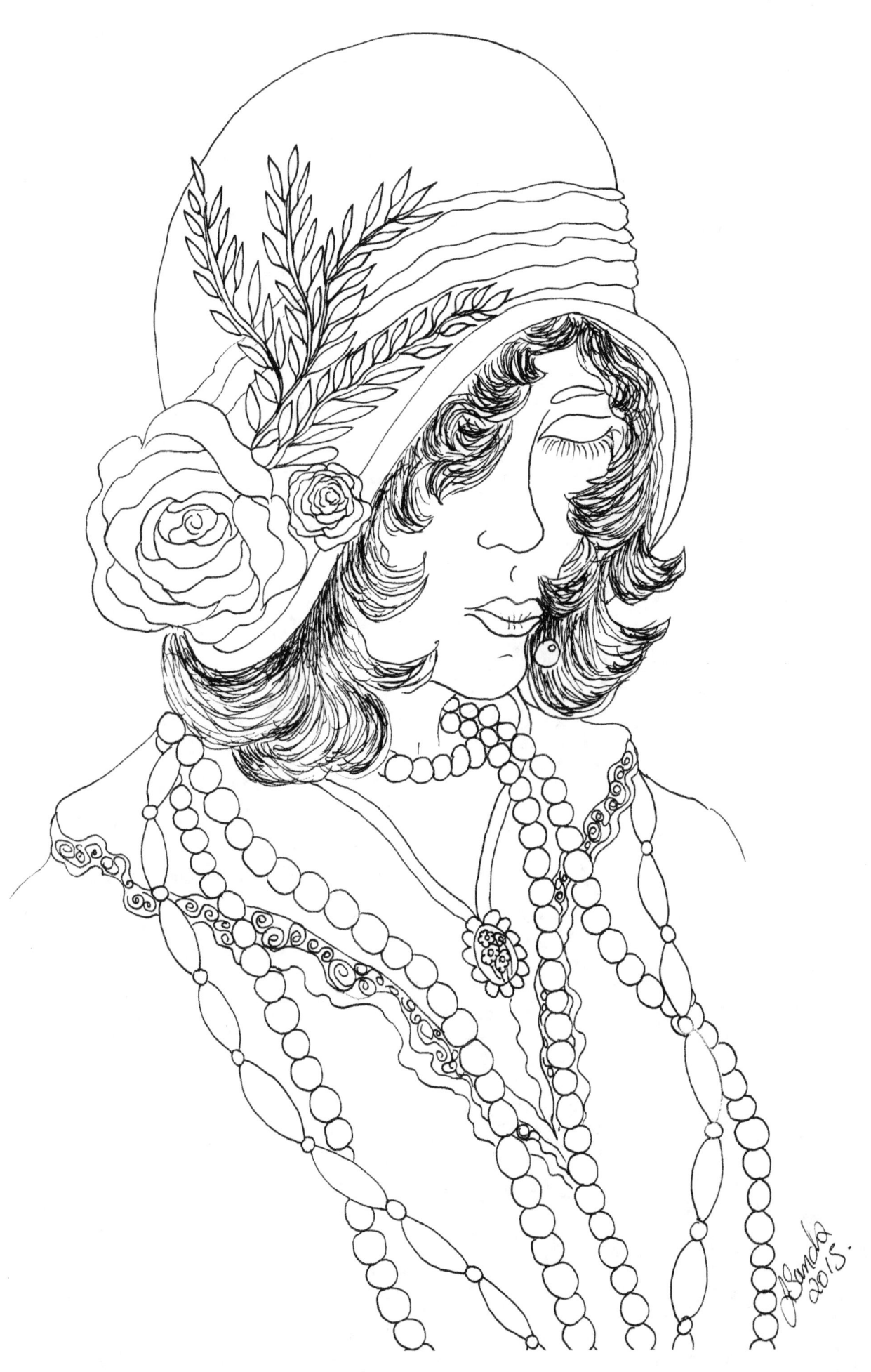

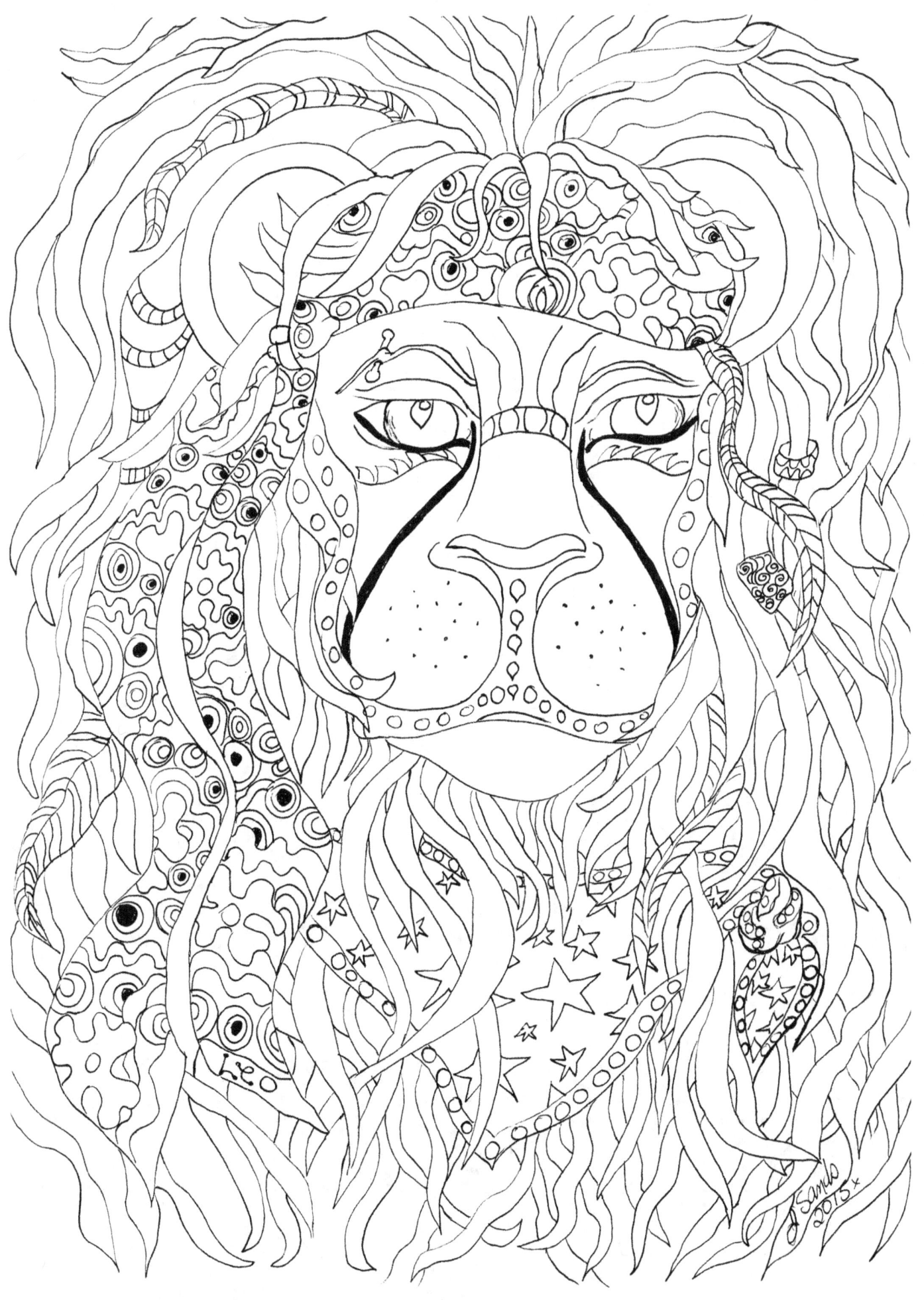

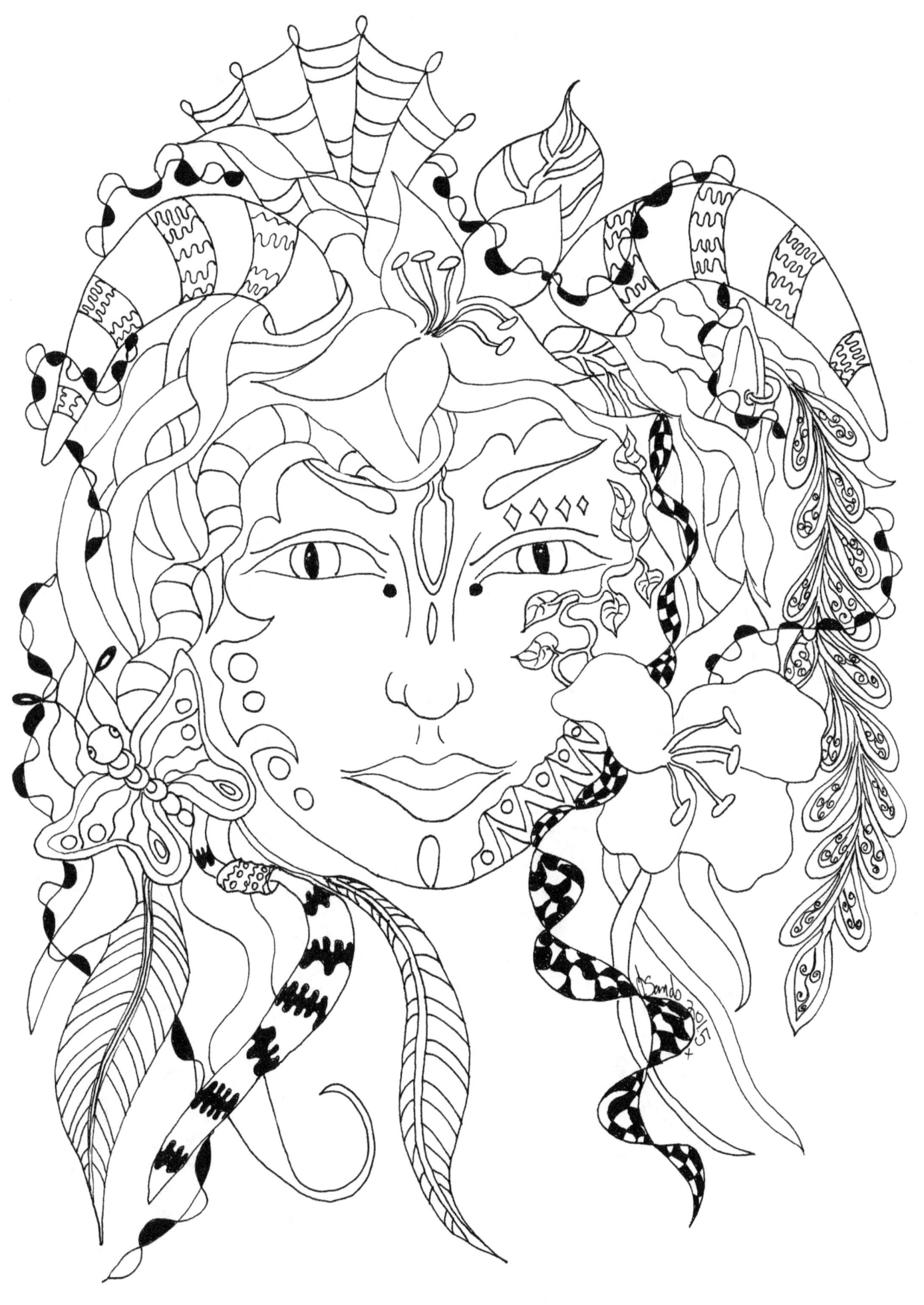

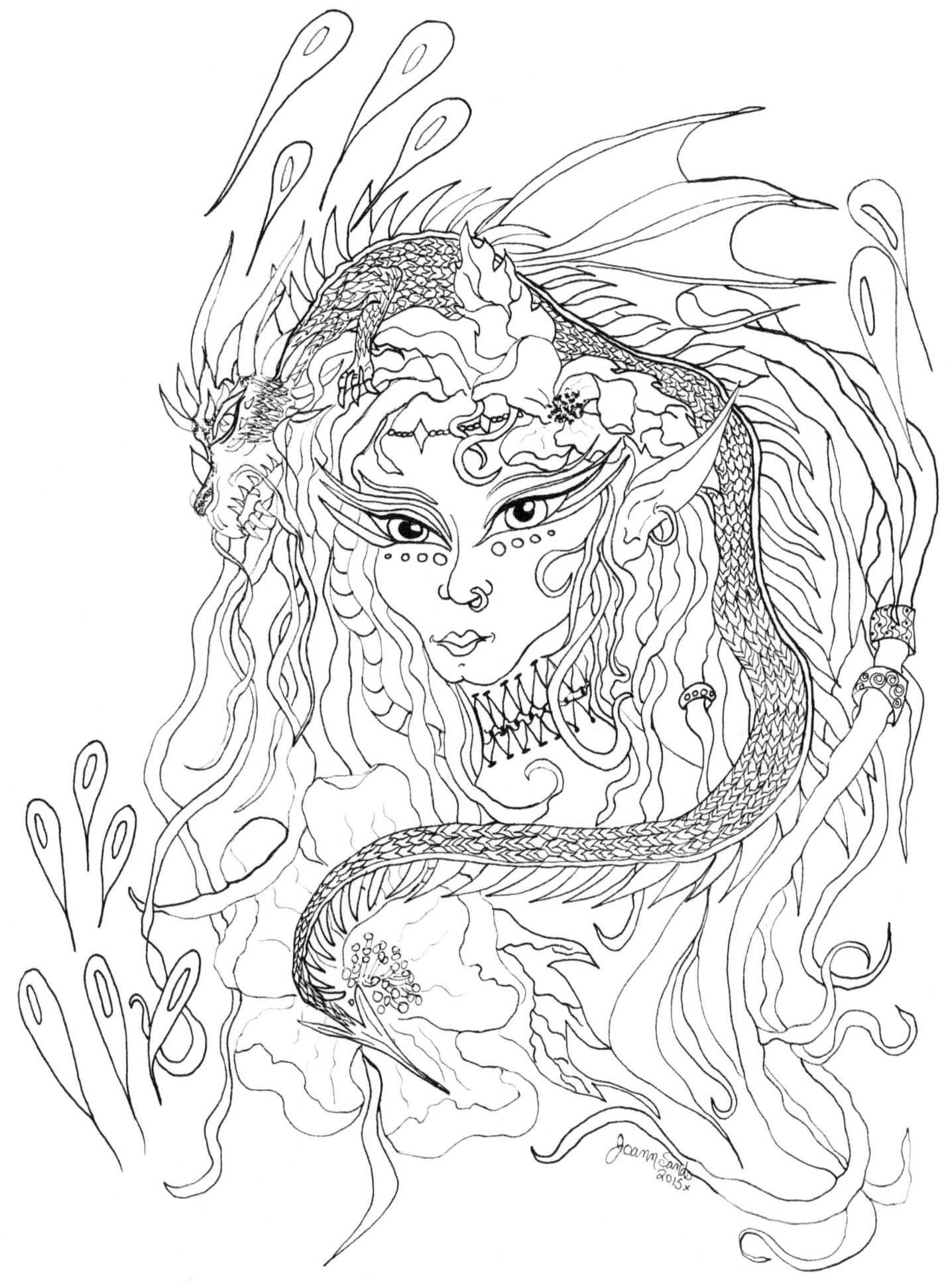

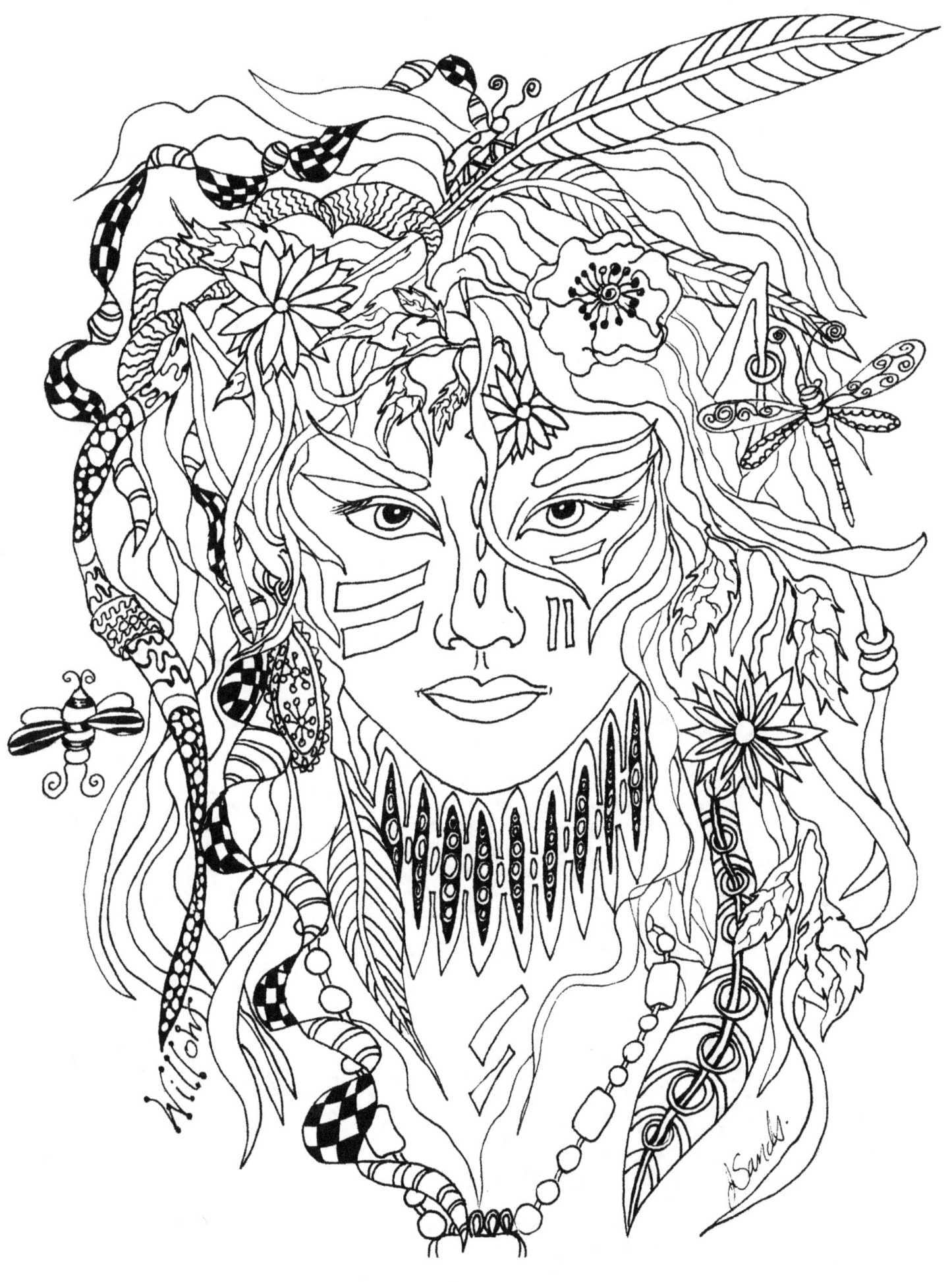

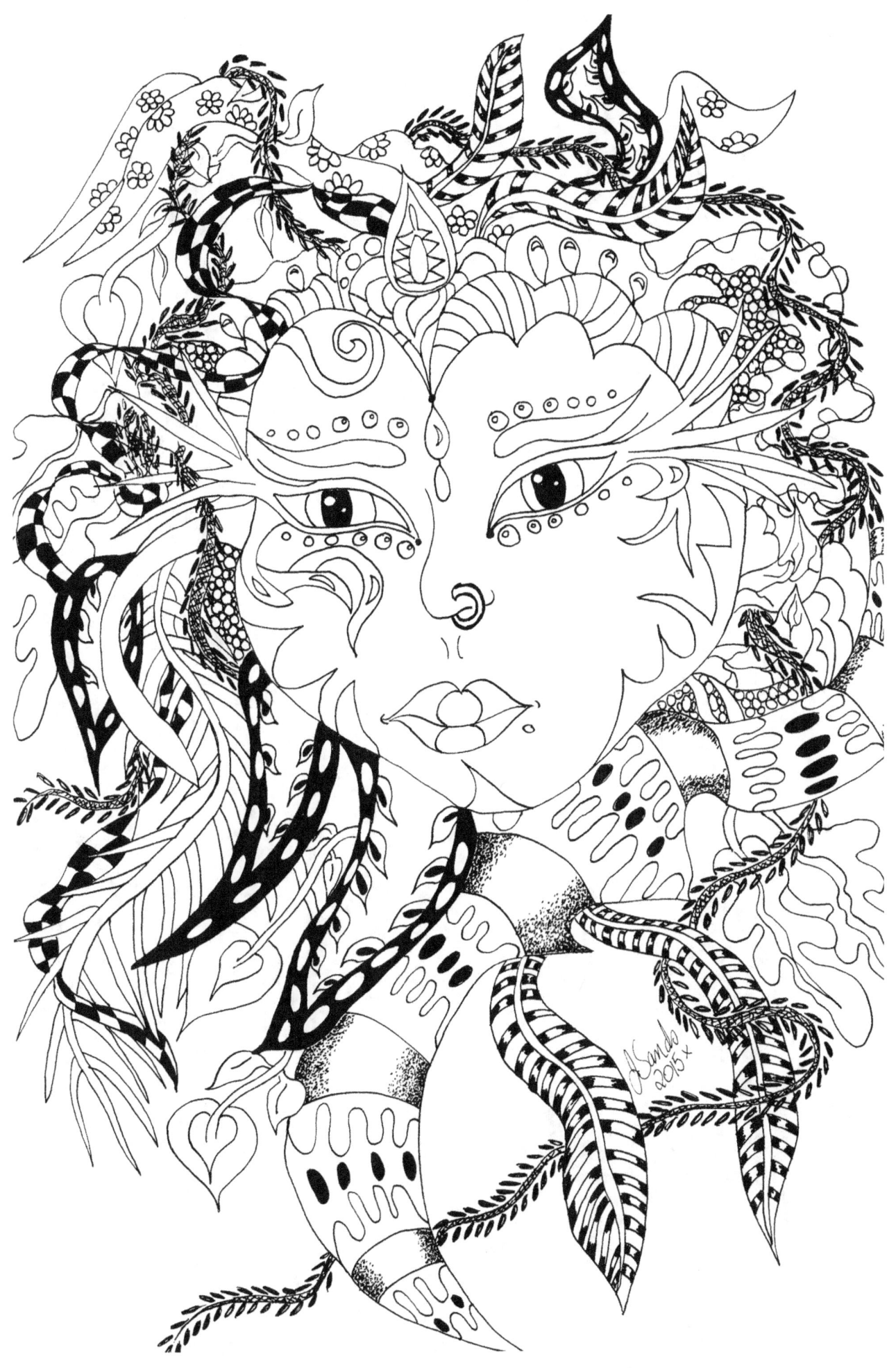

Chapter 7
Fabienne Tosi
Switzerland

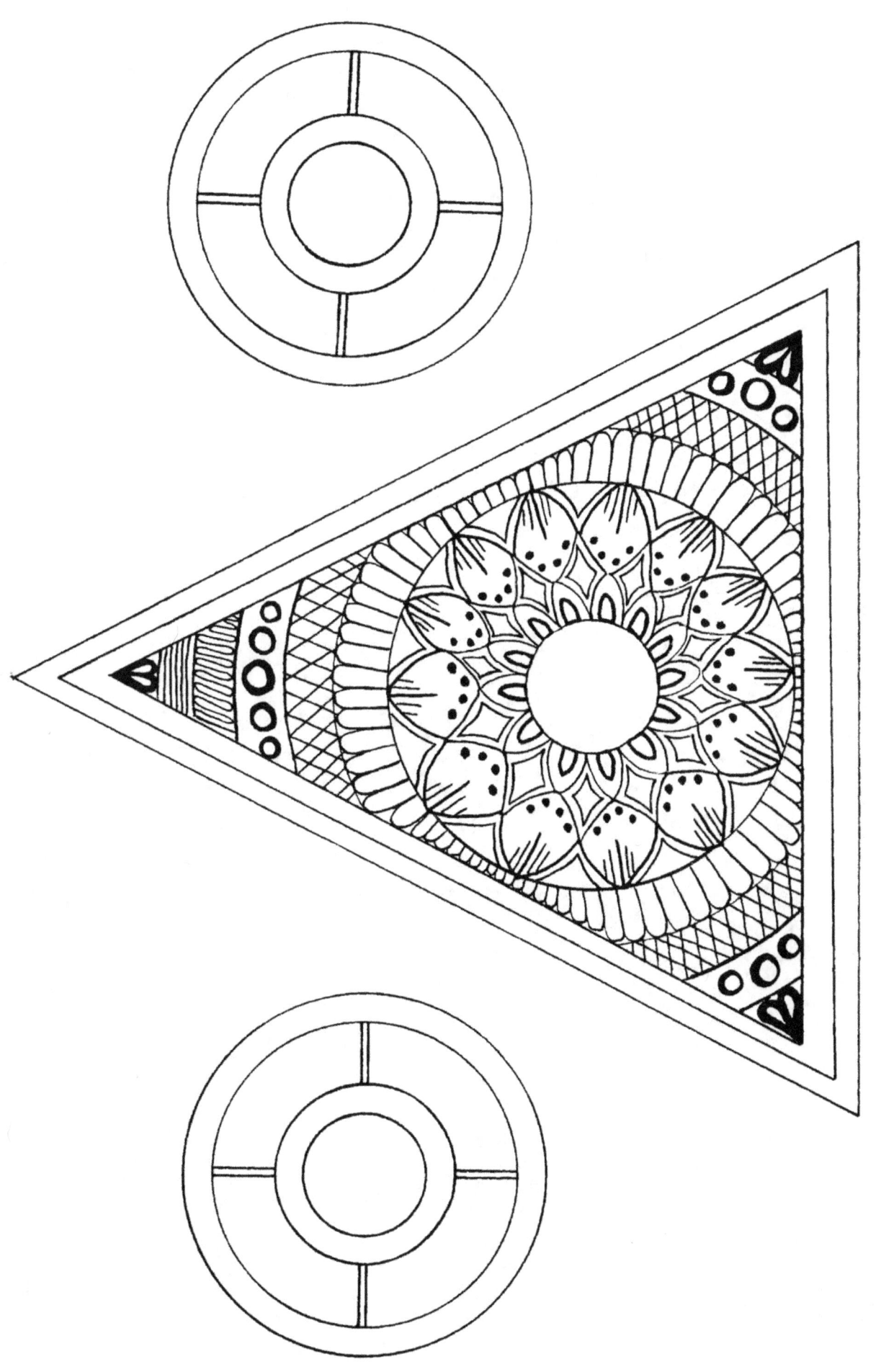

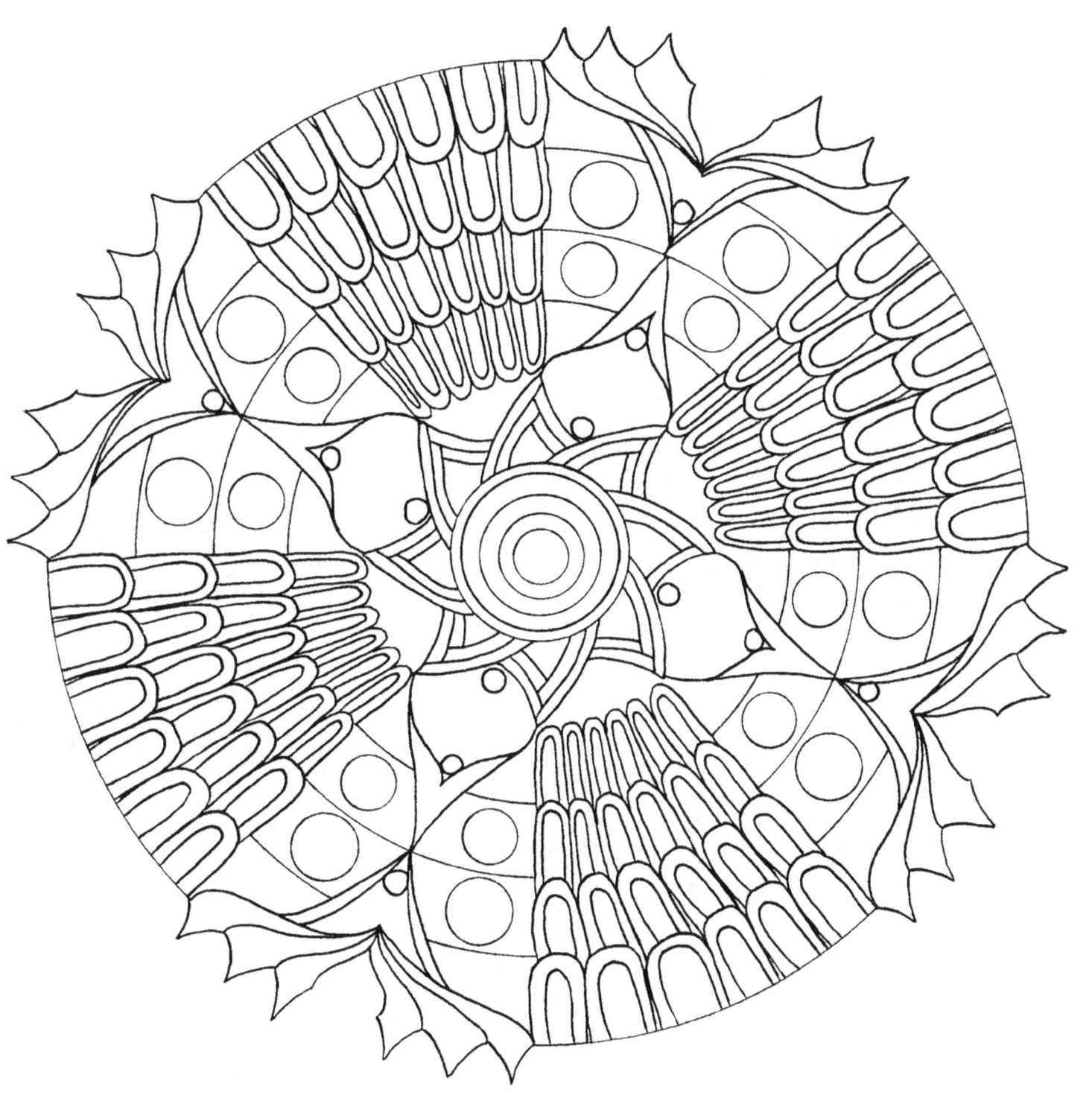

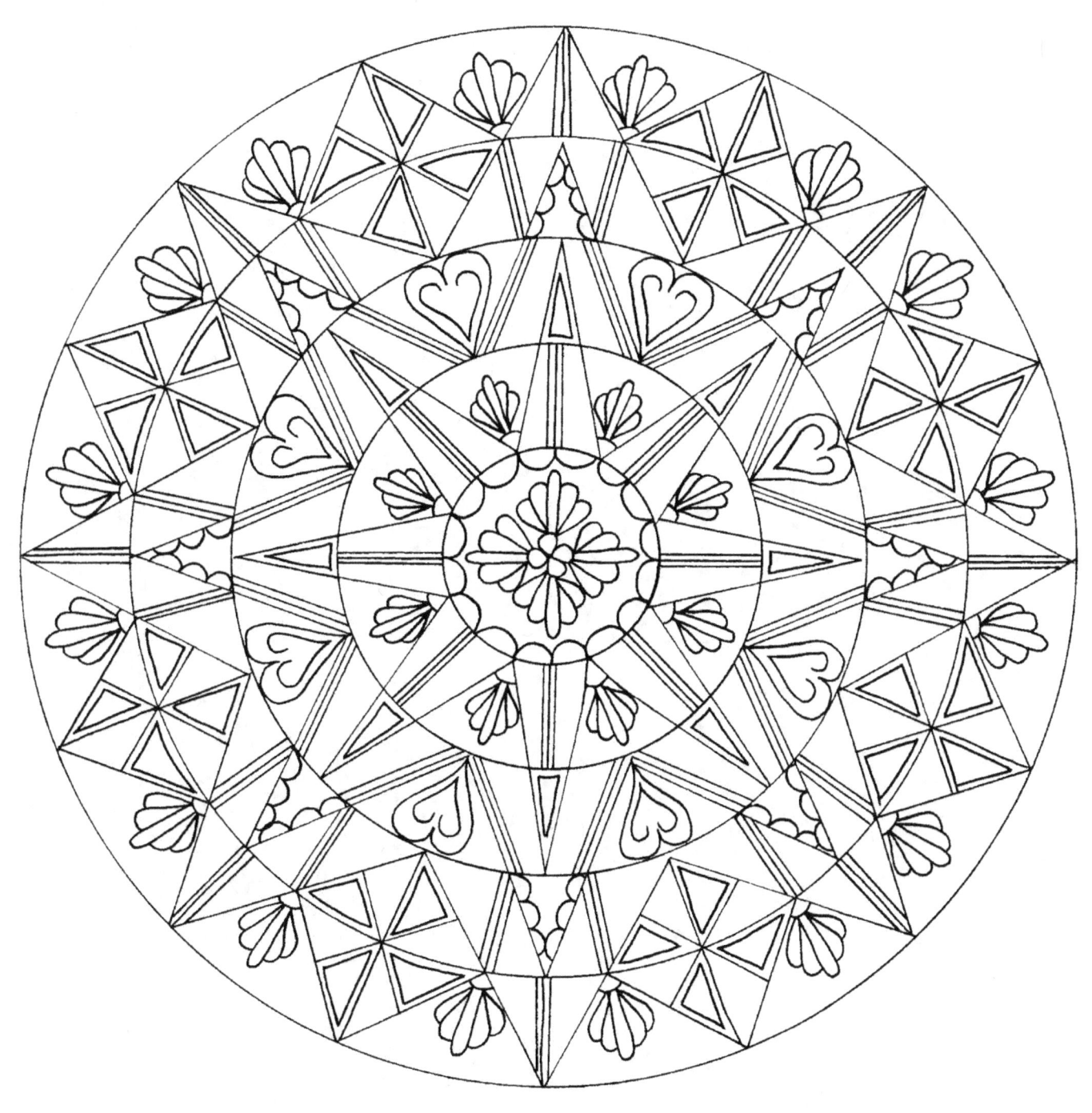

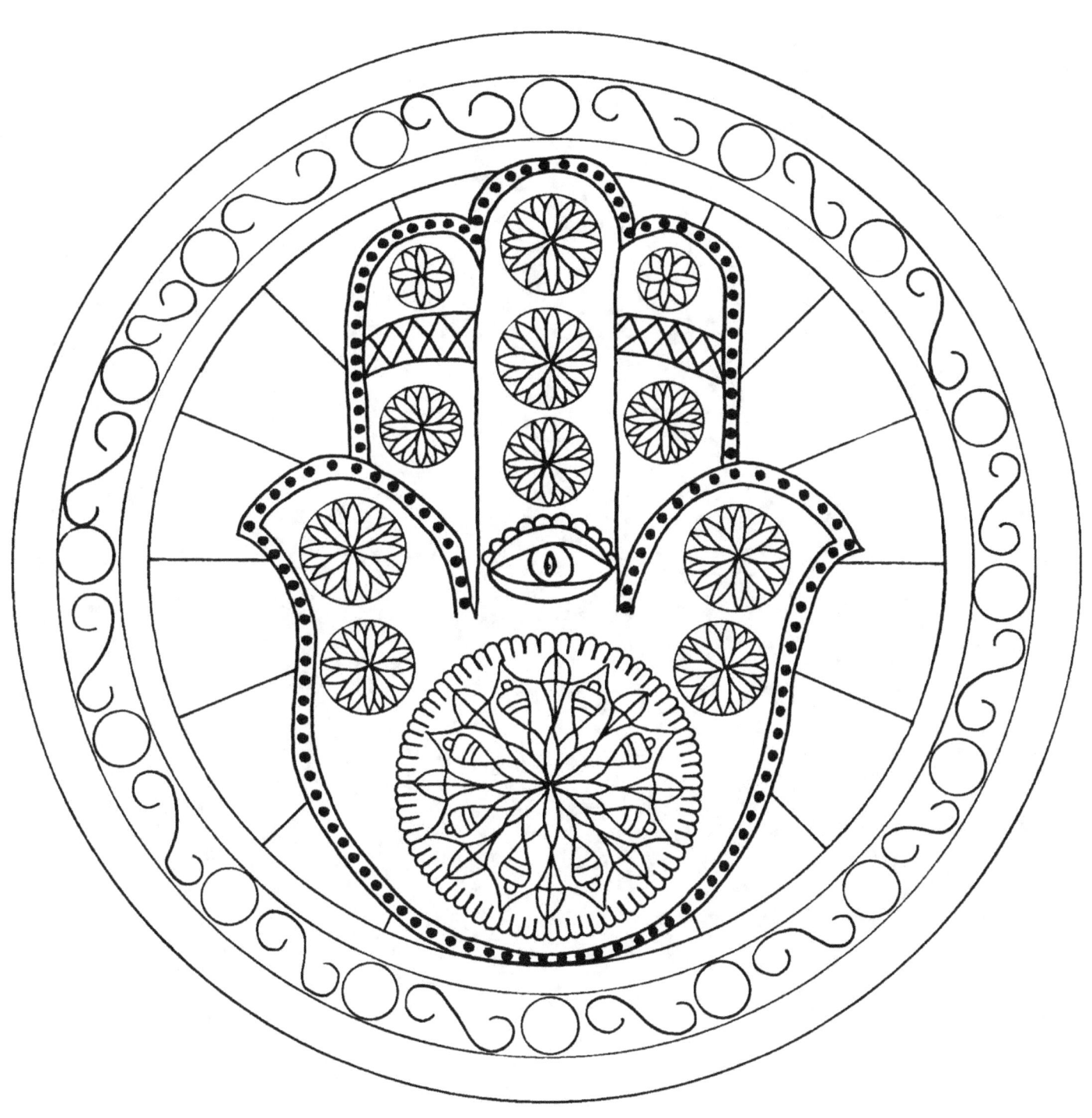

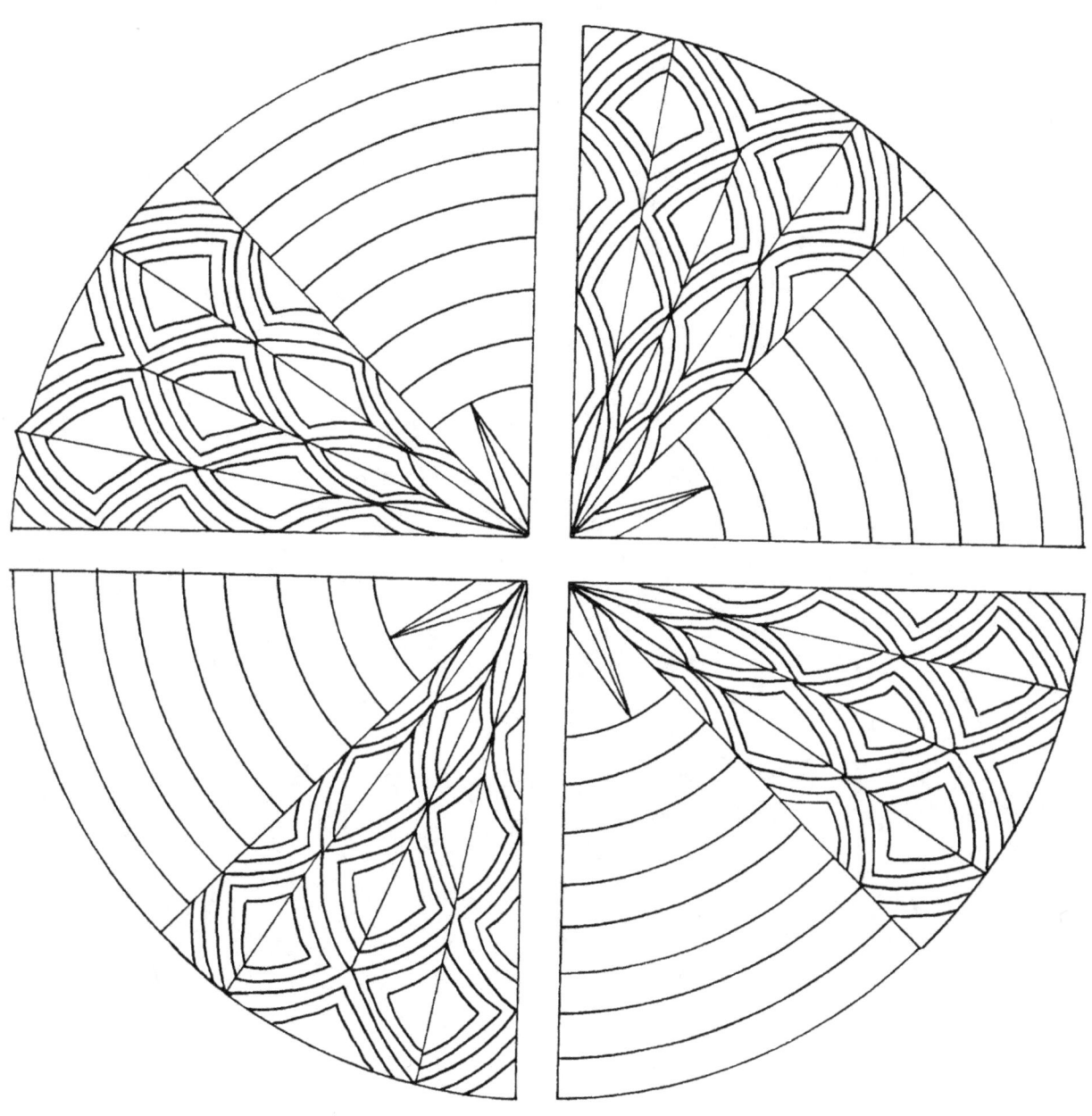

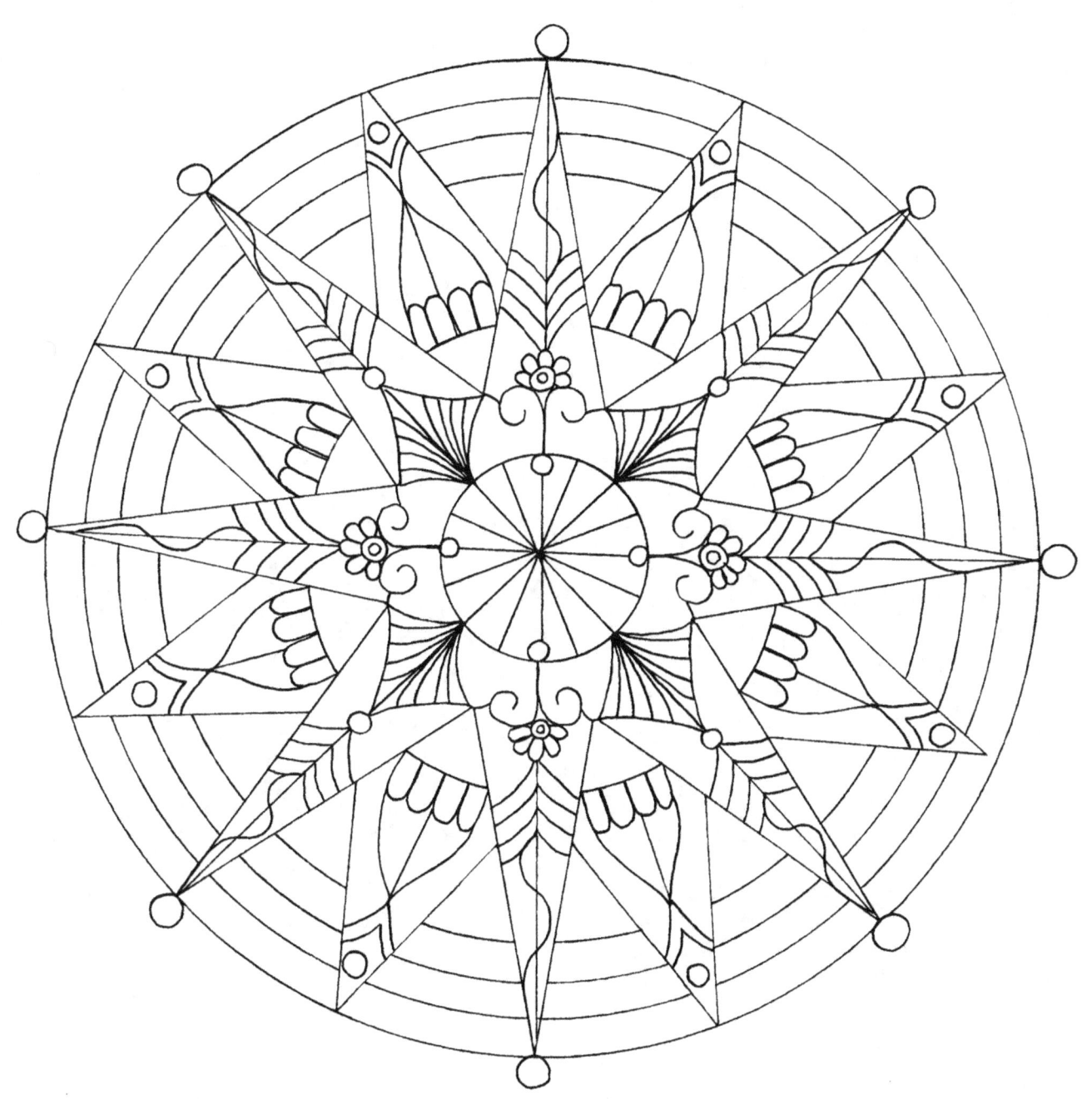

Chapter 8
Asma Zergui
Egypt

Facebook : Asma-Zergui

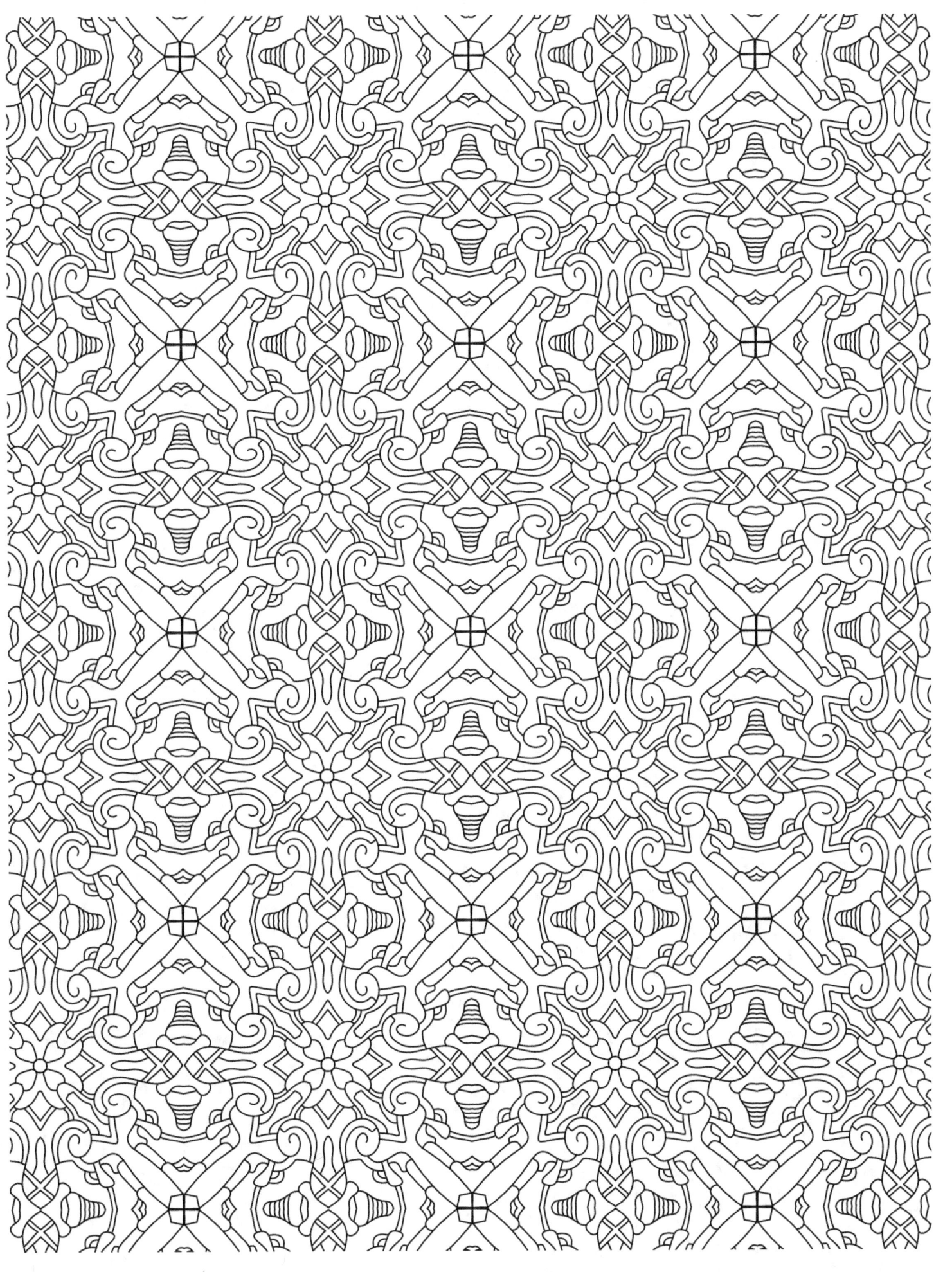

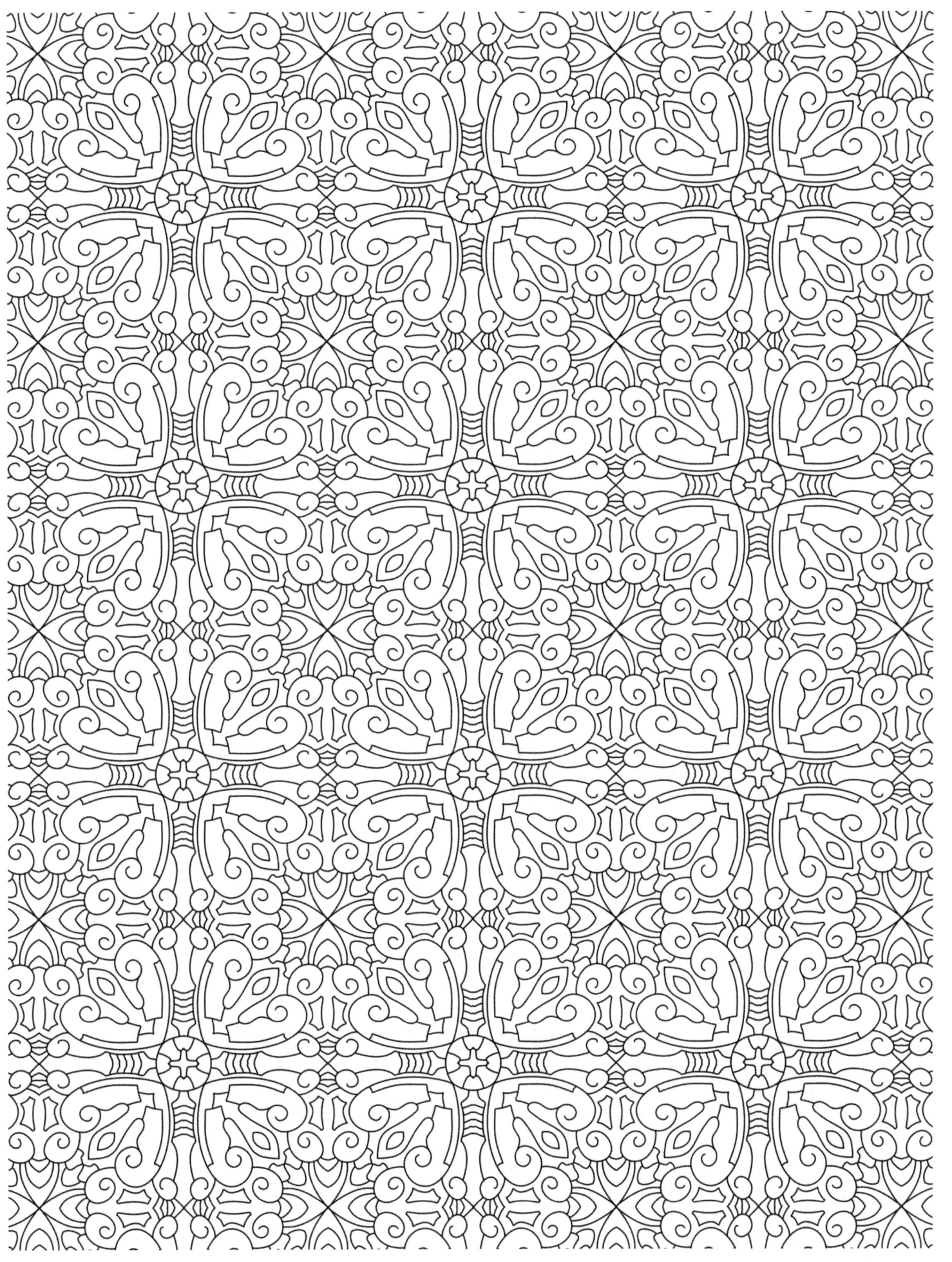

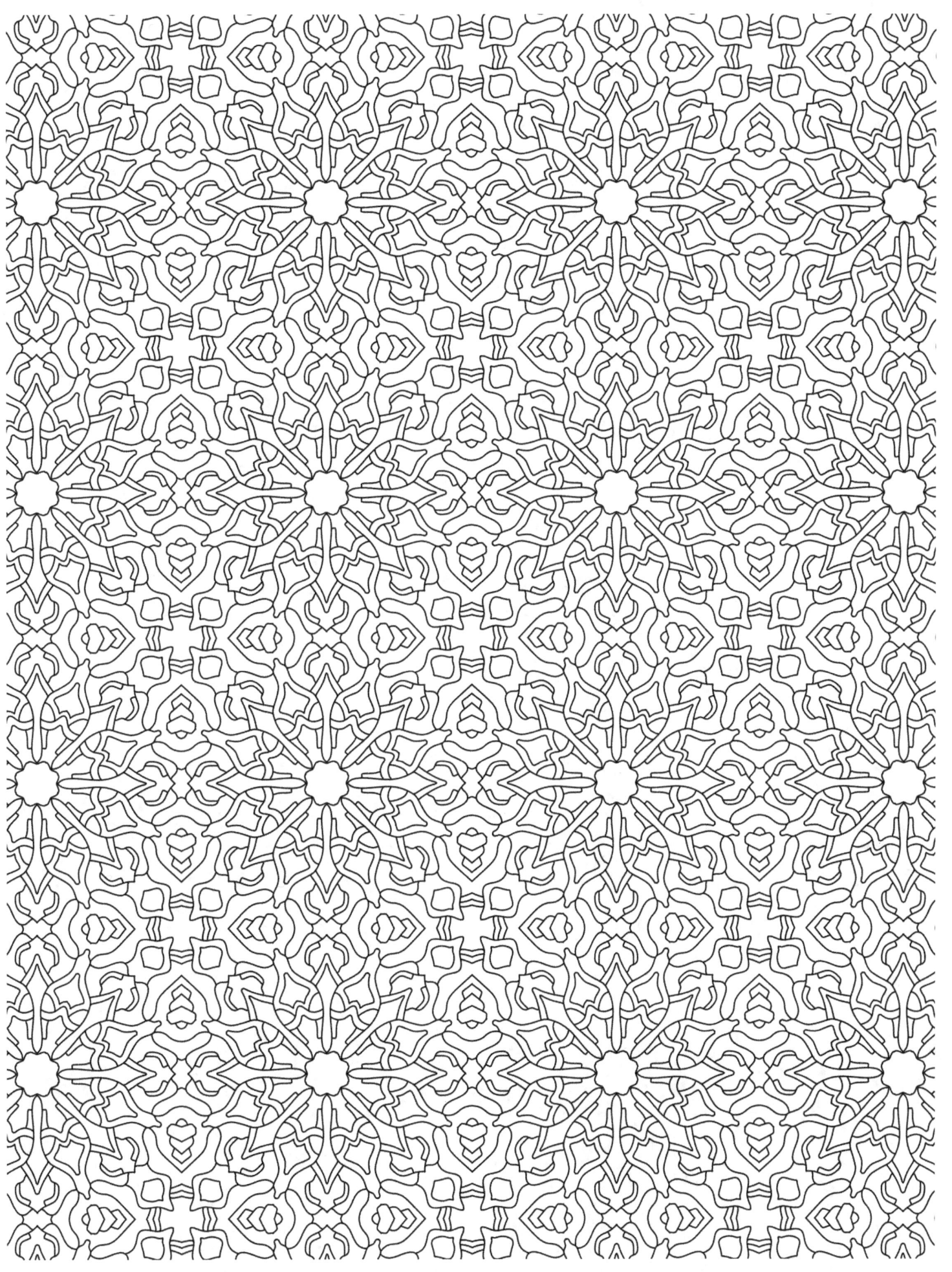

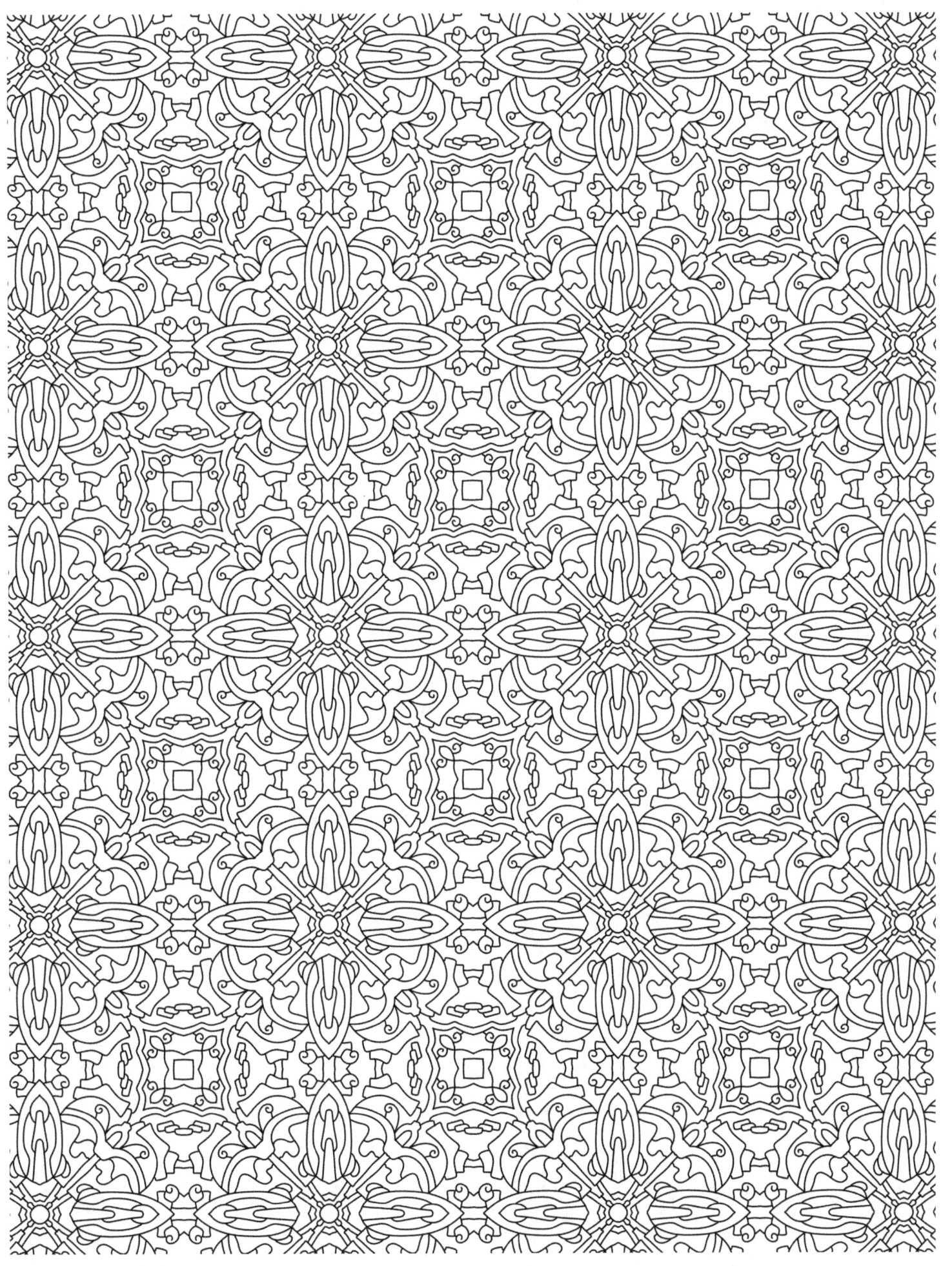

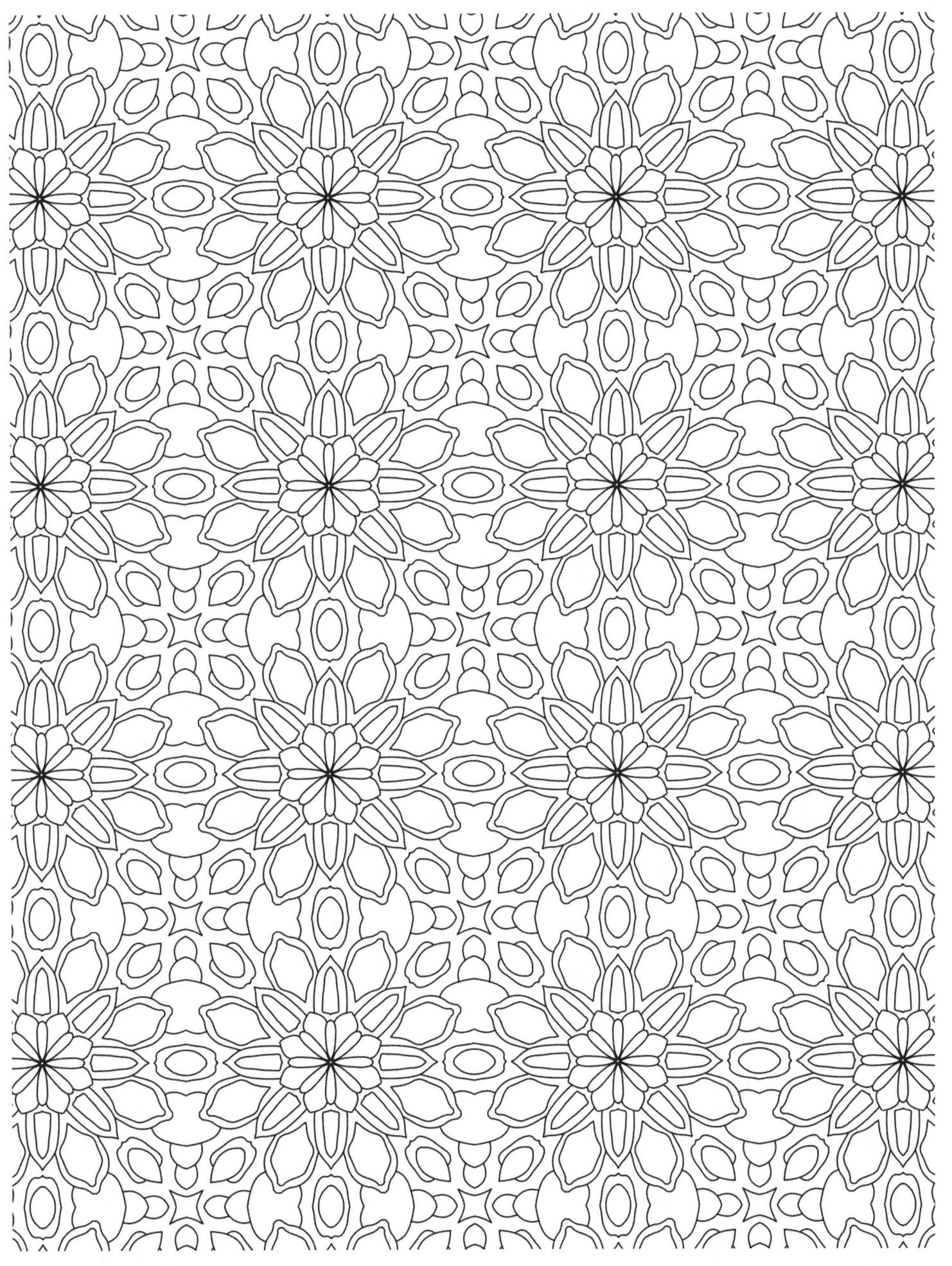

Chapter 9
Mireille Westerduin
The Netherlands

Facebook : Colourbymi

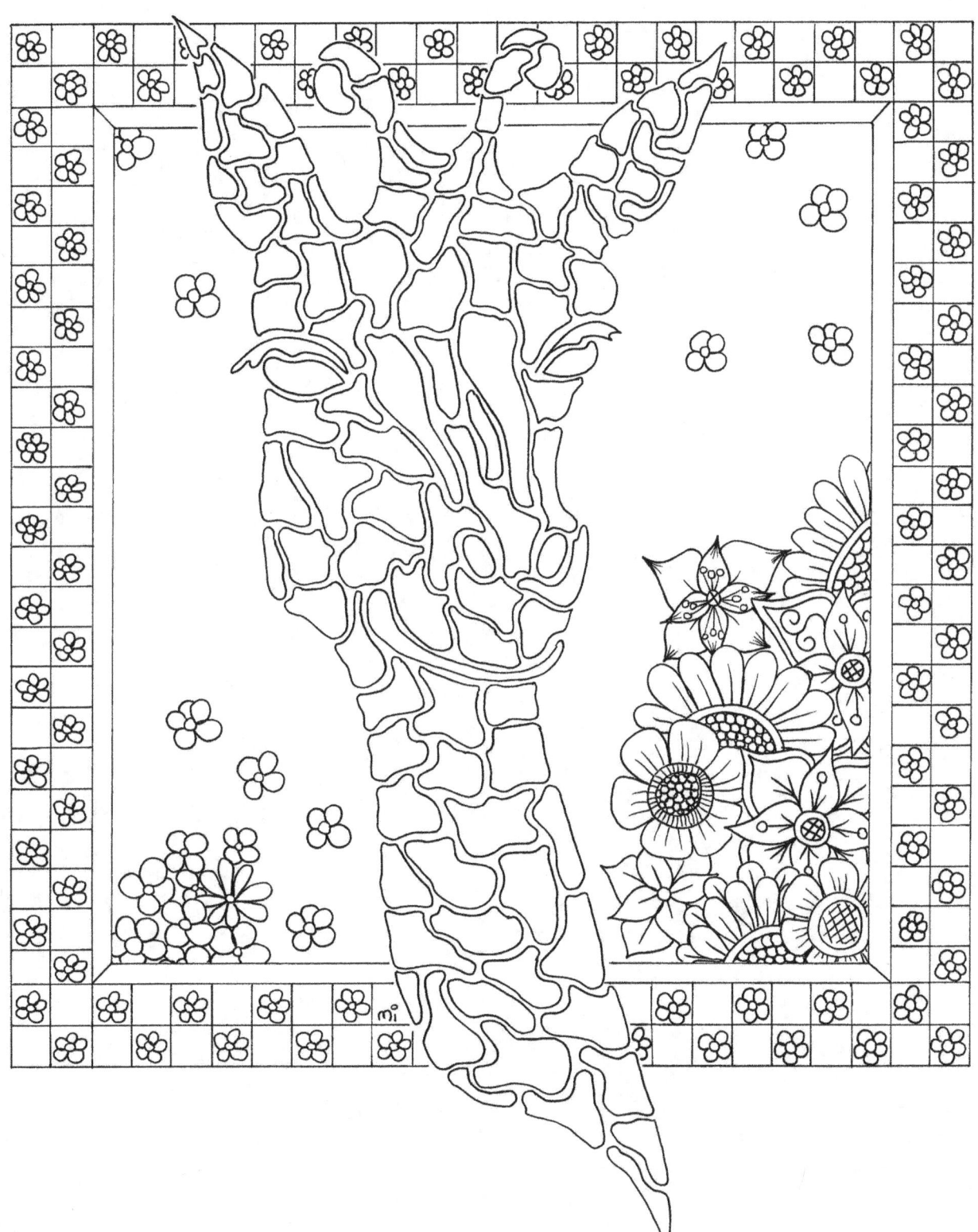

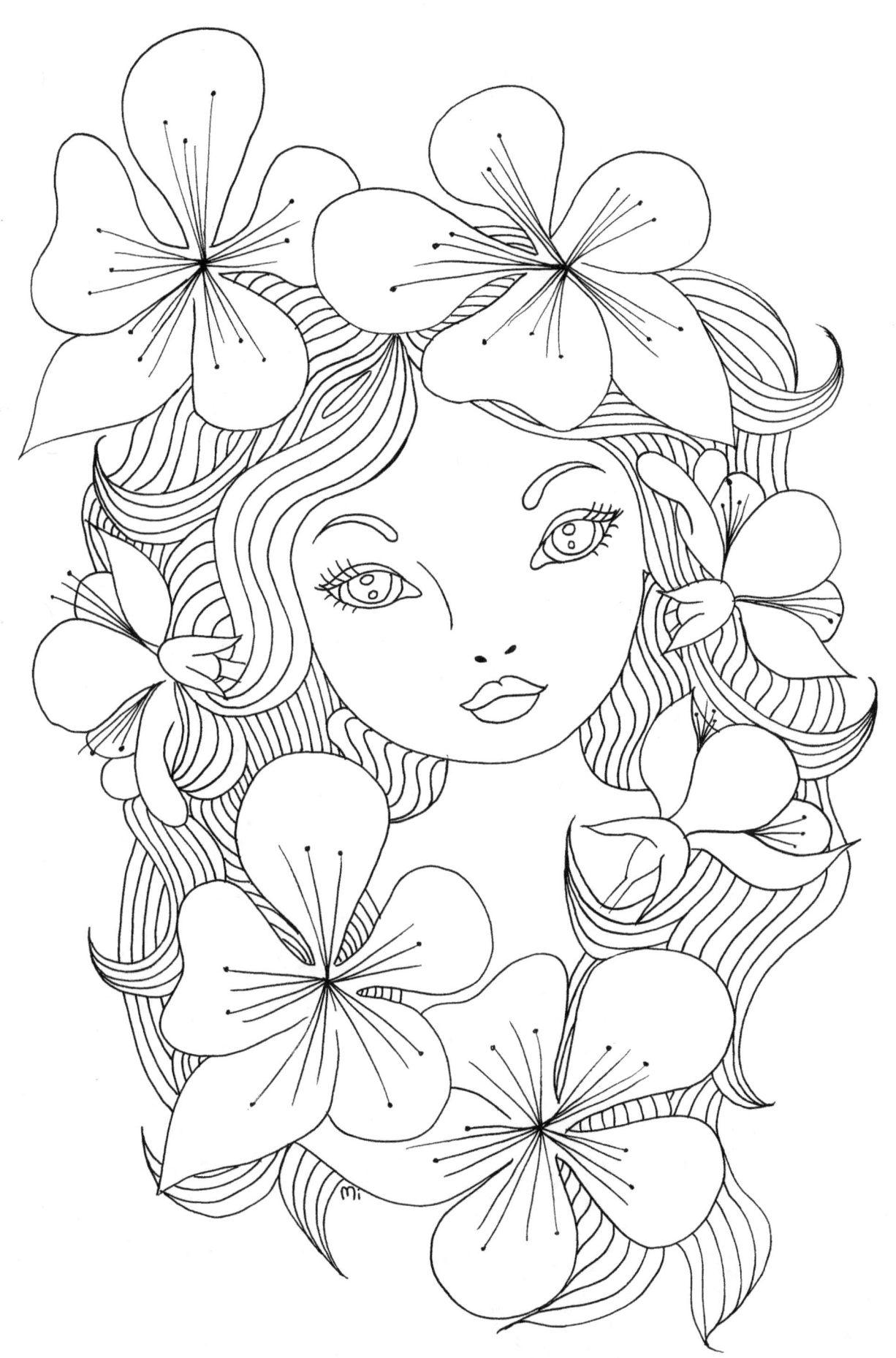

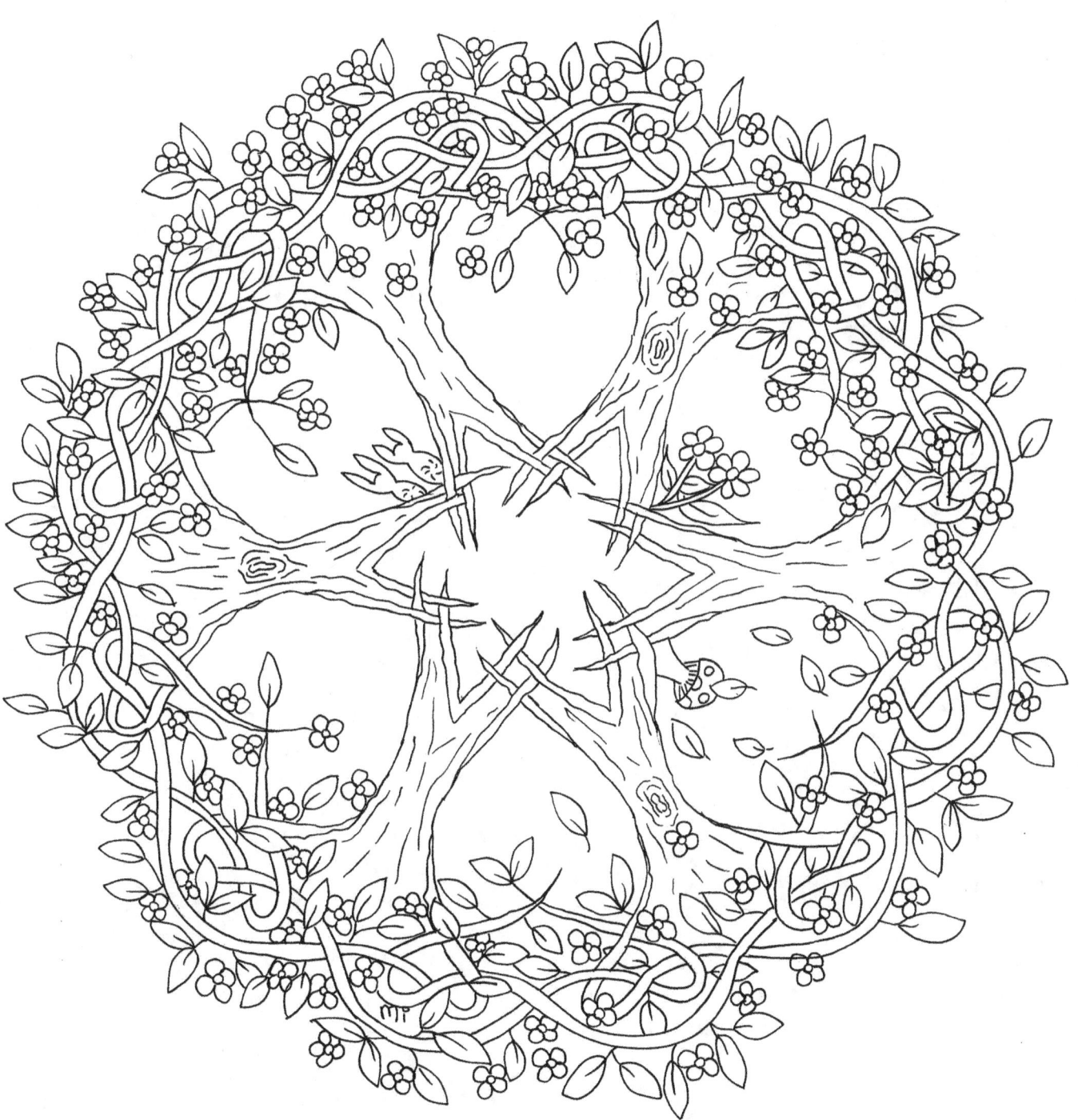

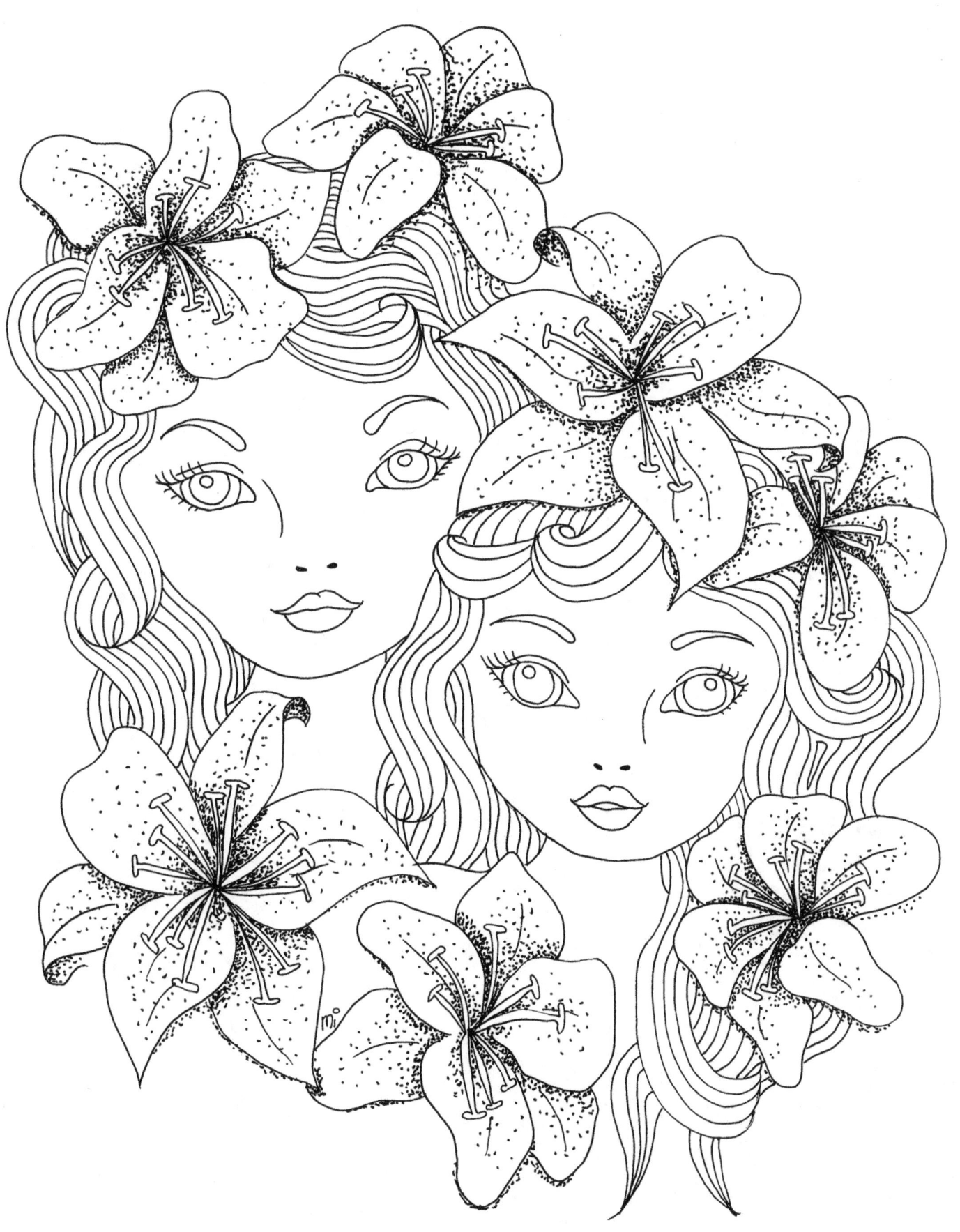

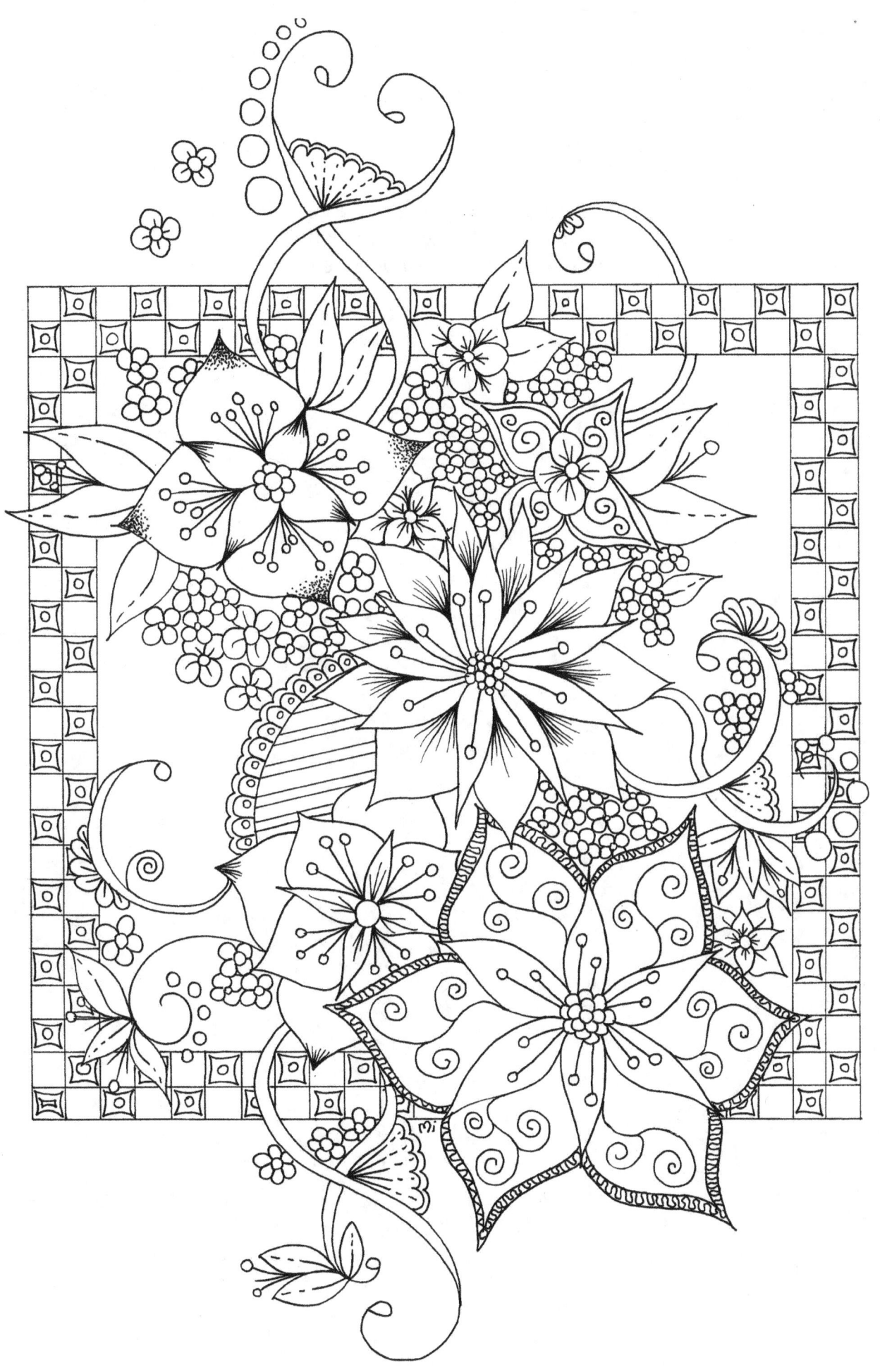

Chapter 10
M. Lin
Taiwan

Facebook : maggiezentangle
Facebook: Maggies.Boutique
http://www.maggies-boutique.com

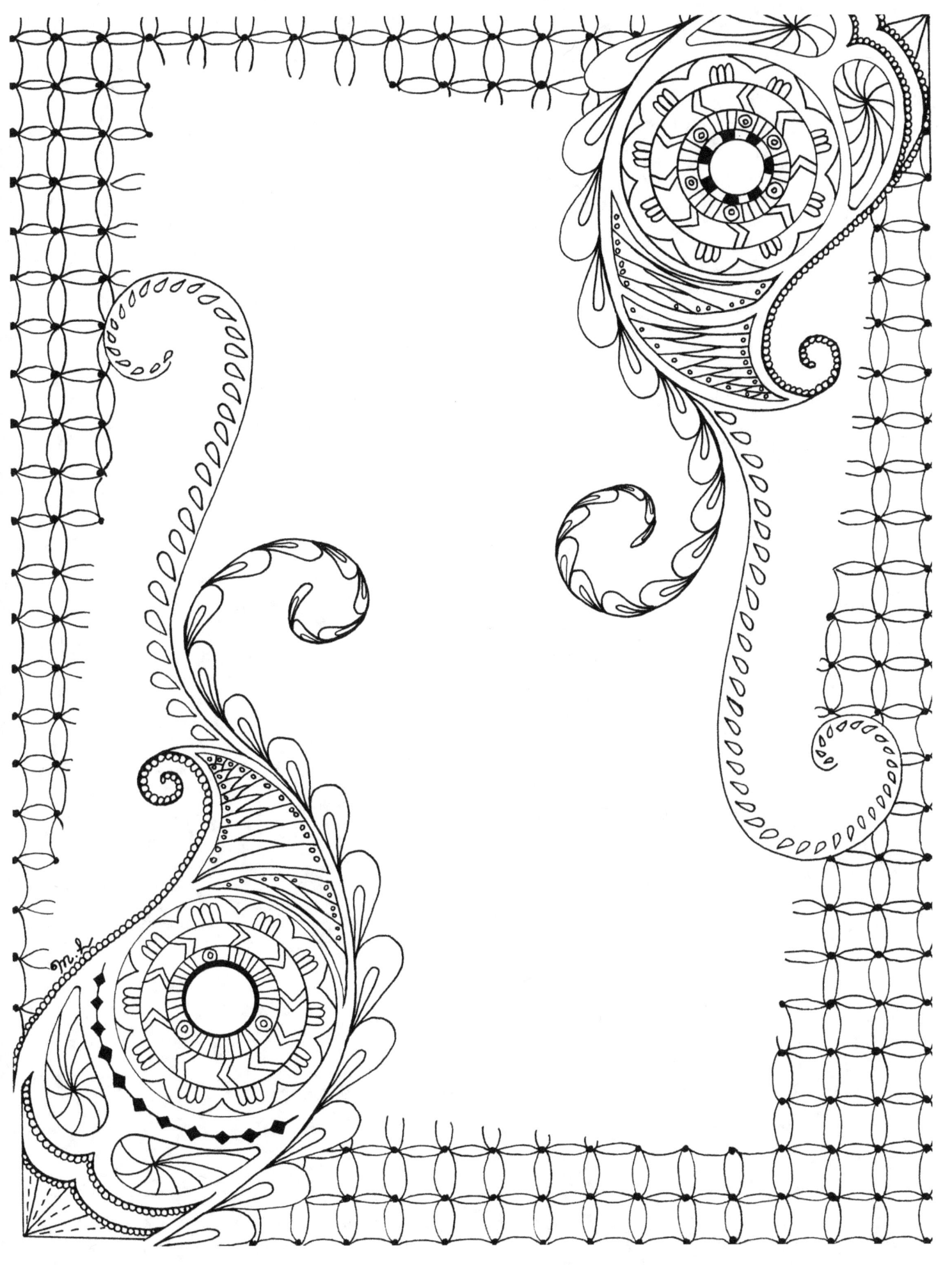

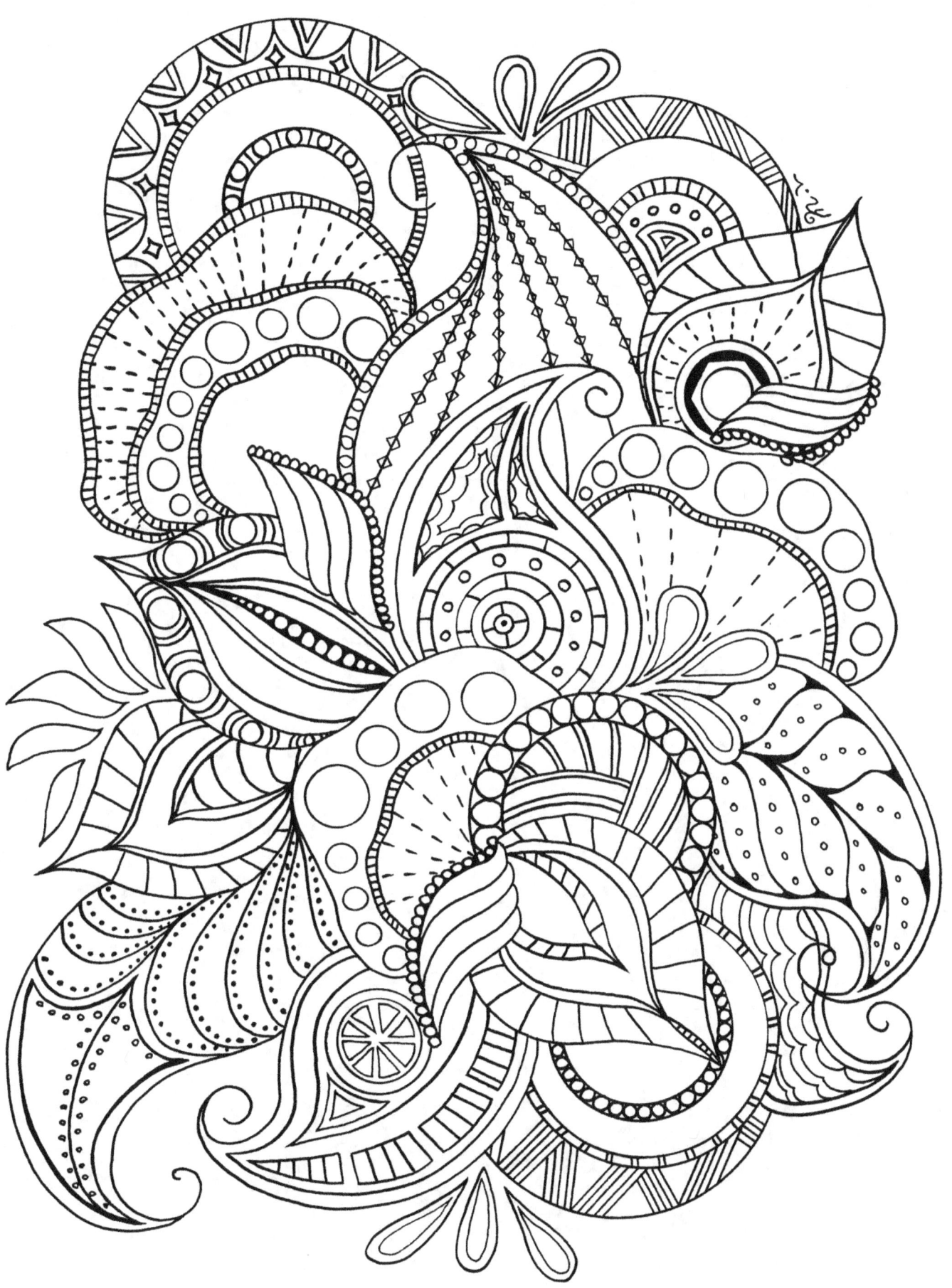

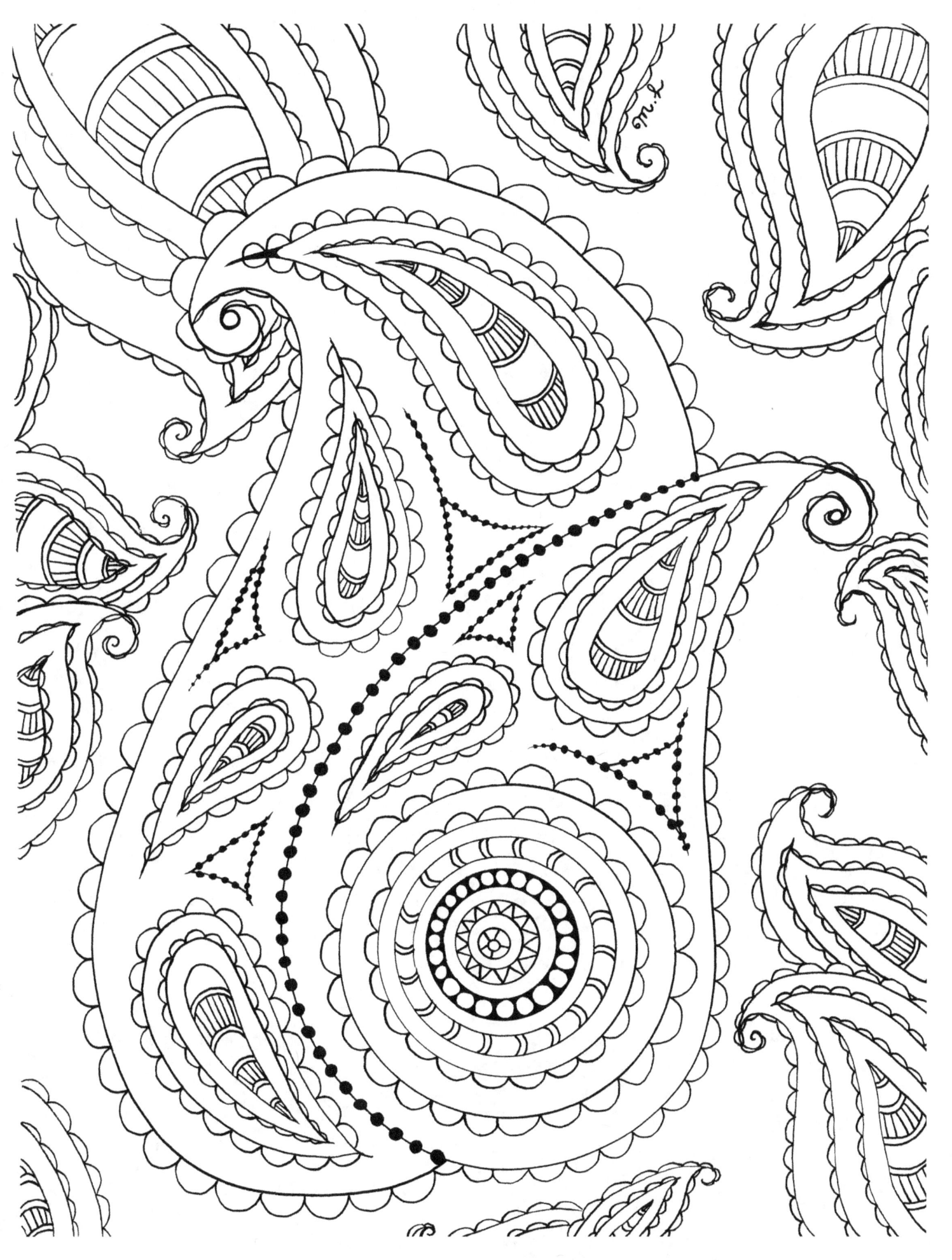

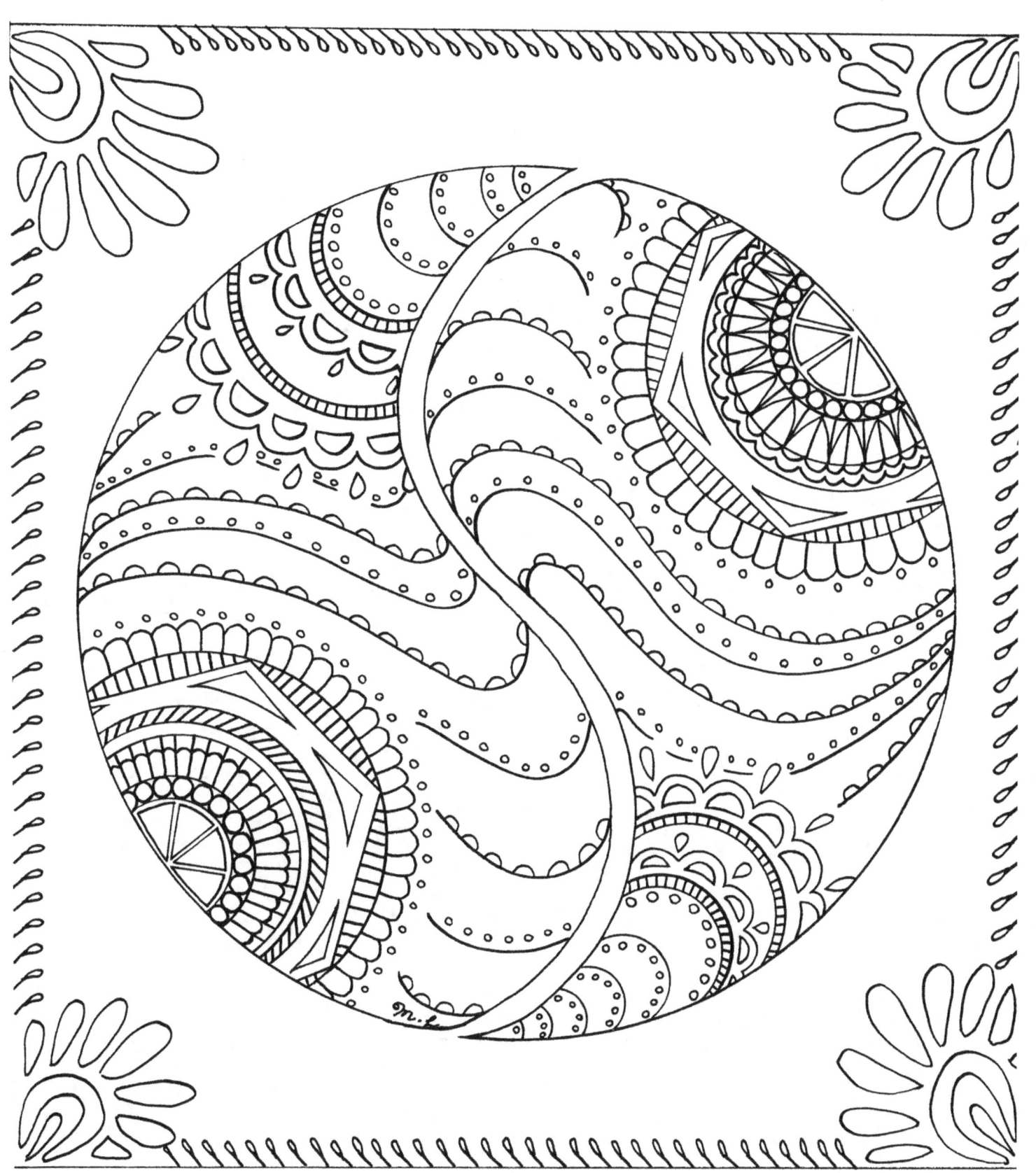

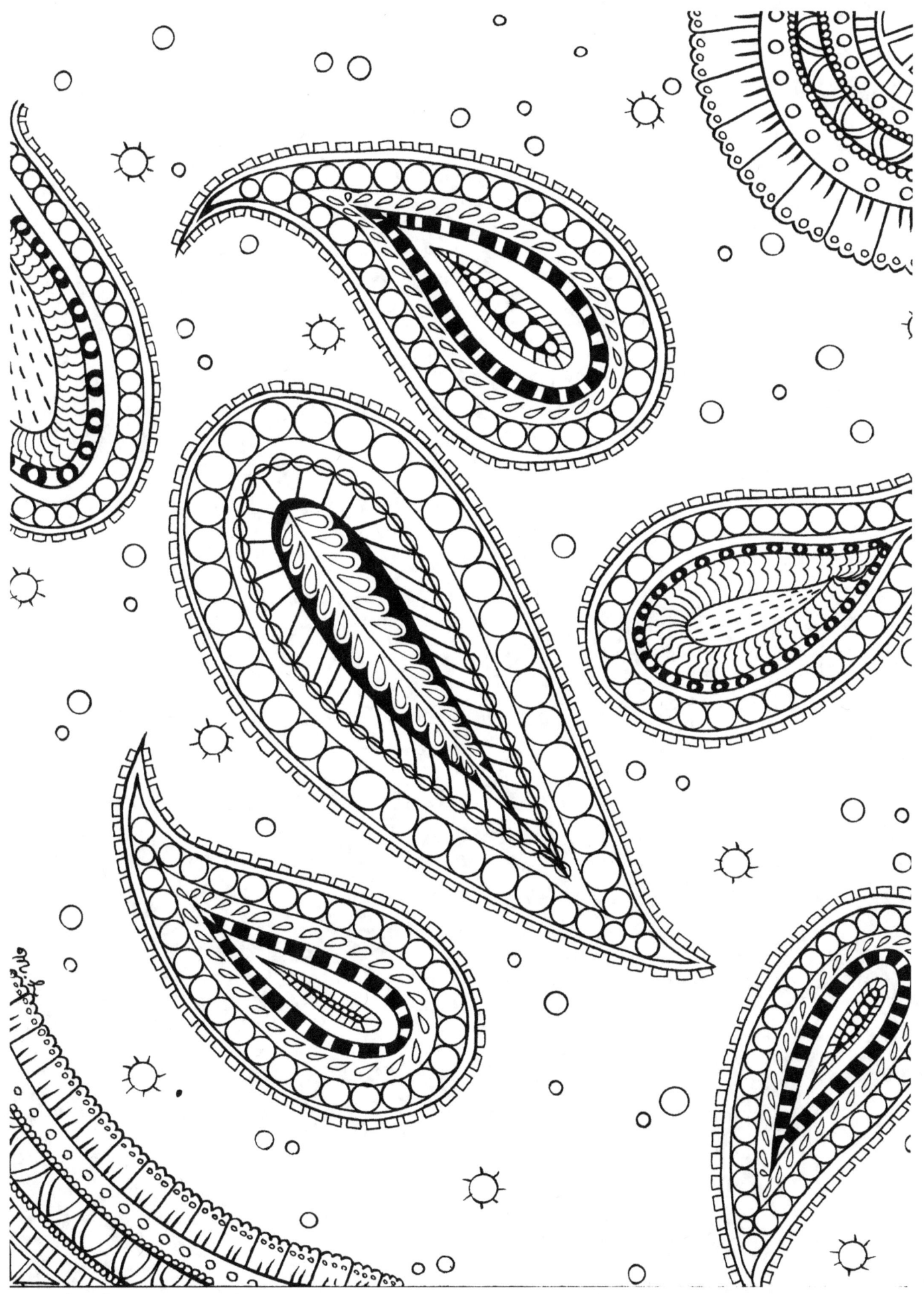

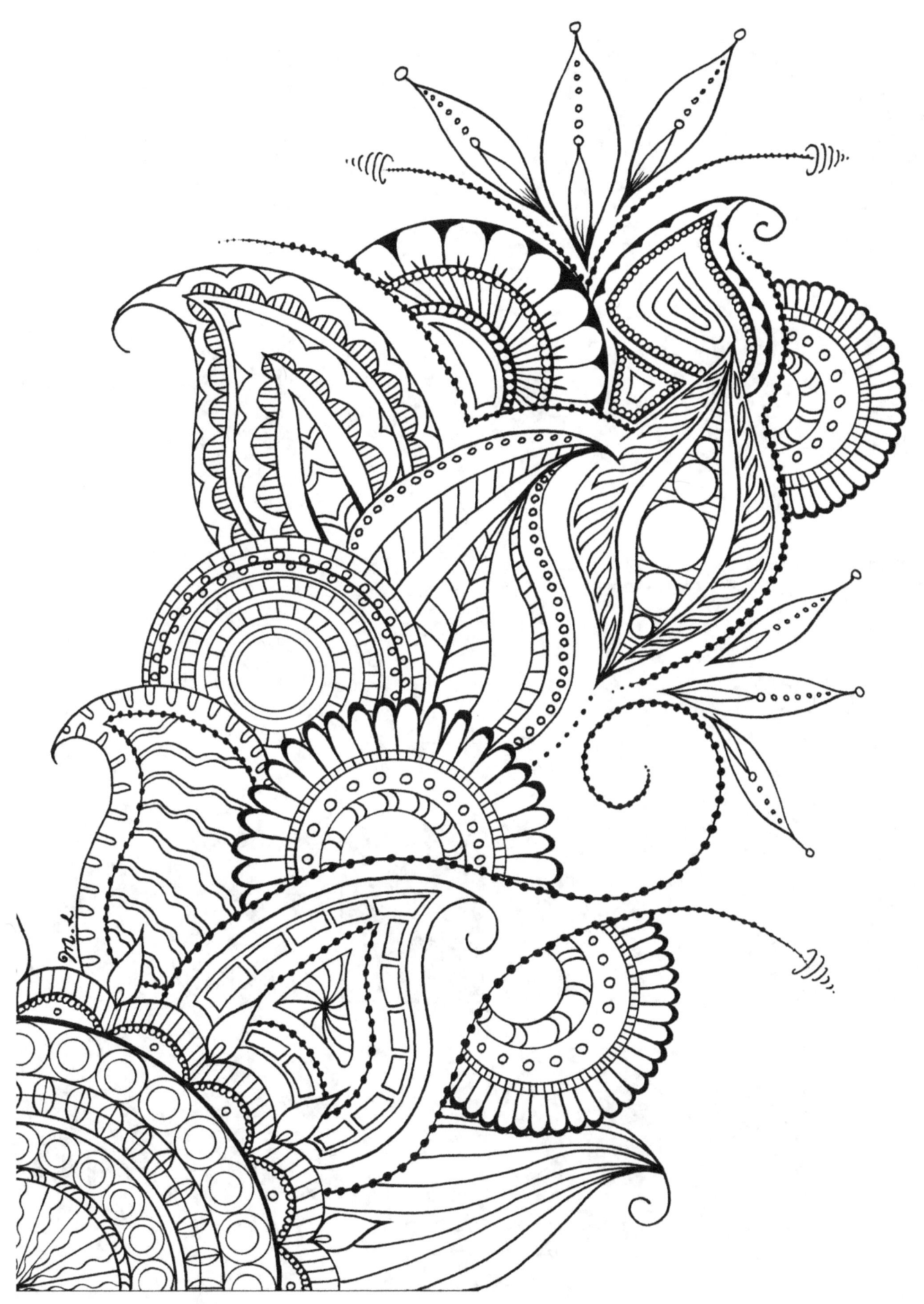

Global Doodle Gems Volume 15 Preview

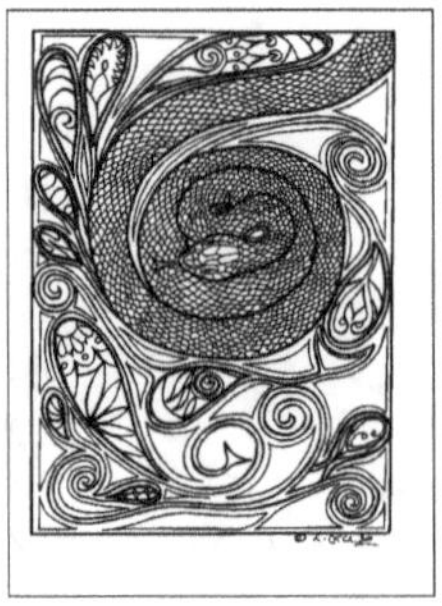

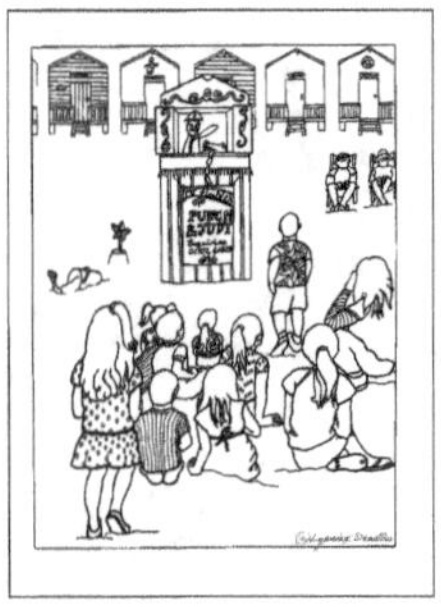

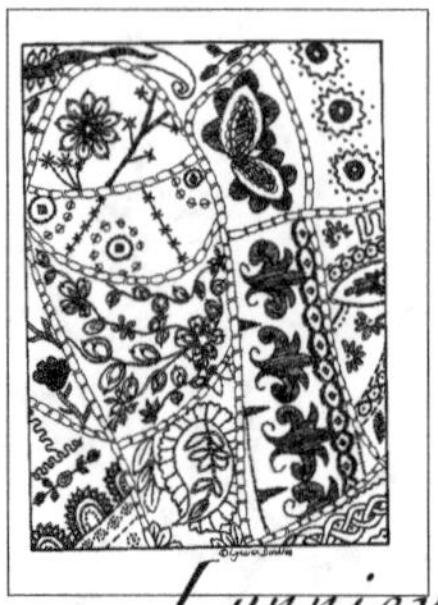

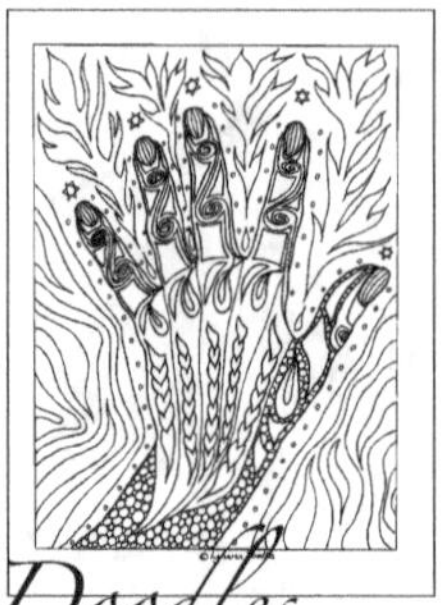

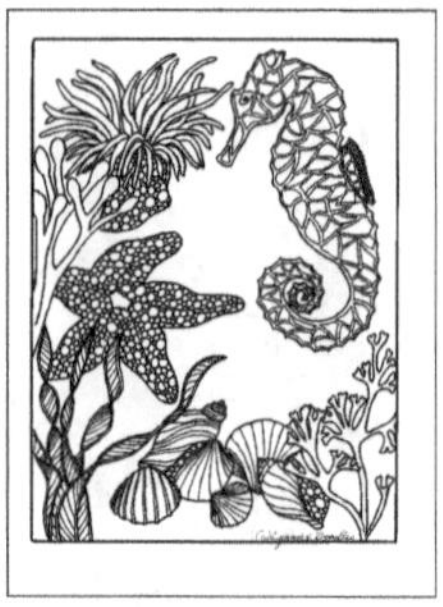

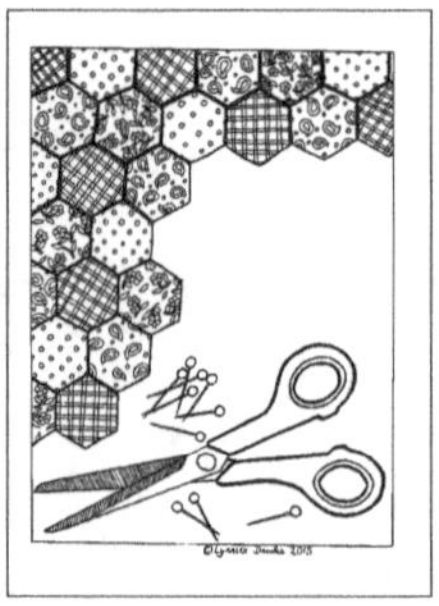

Lynniex Doodles

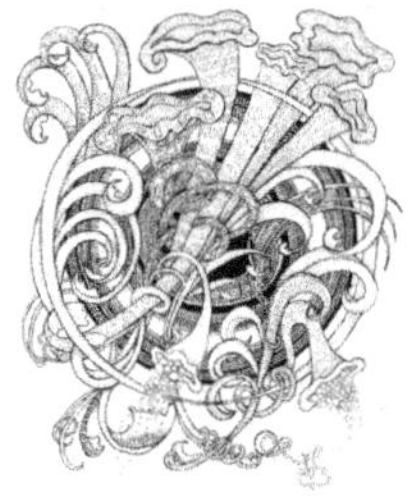

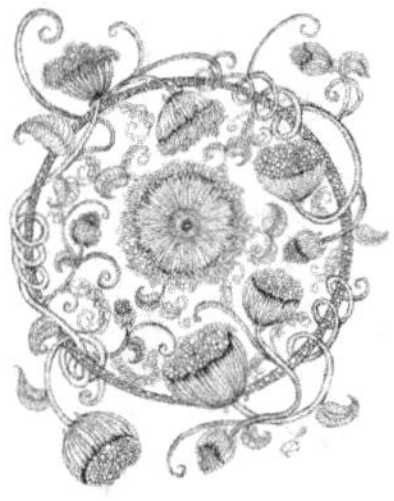

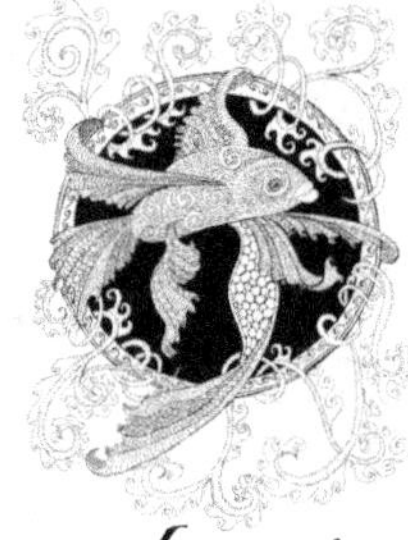

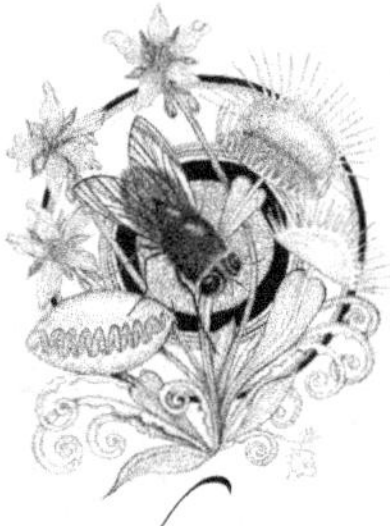

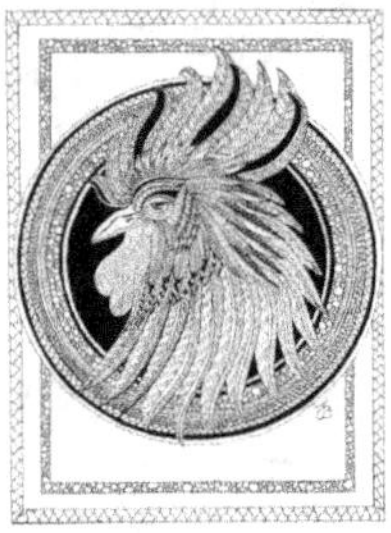

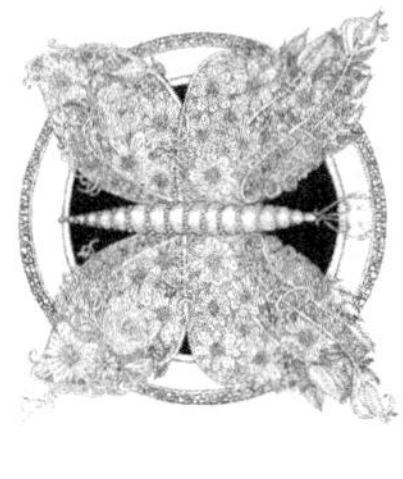

Laurie Beauchamp

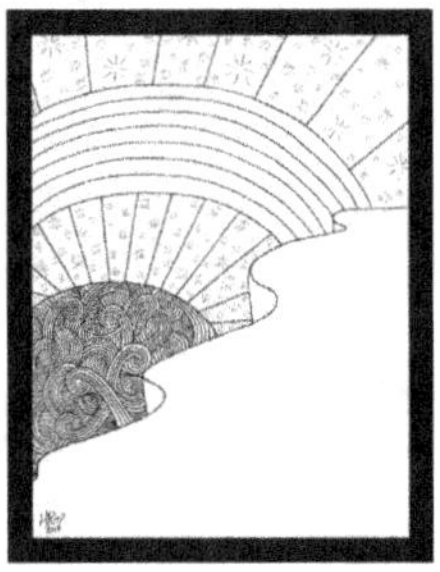

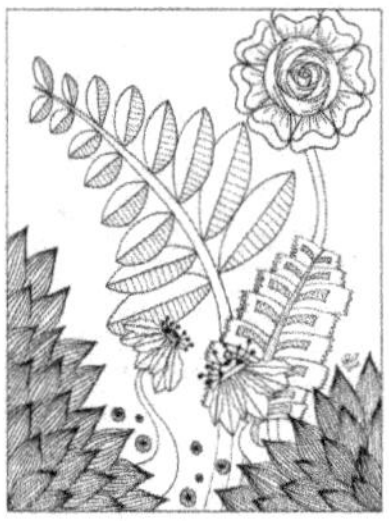

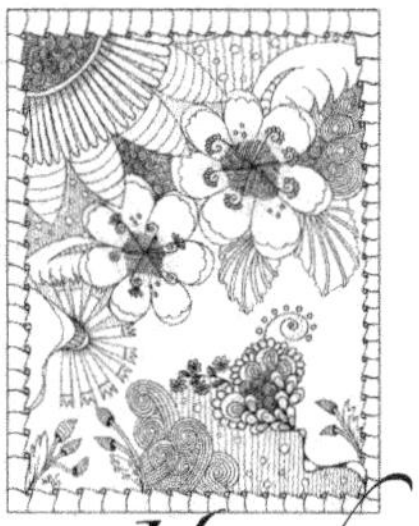

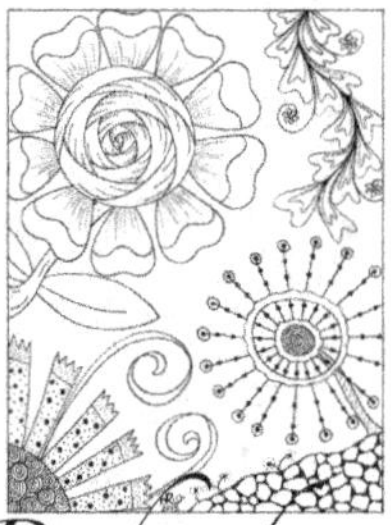

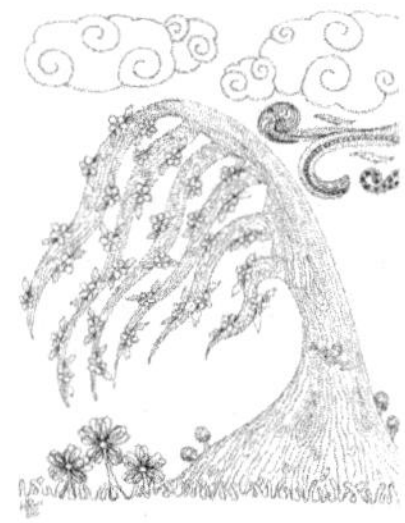

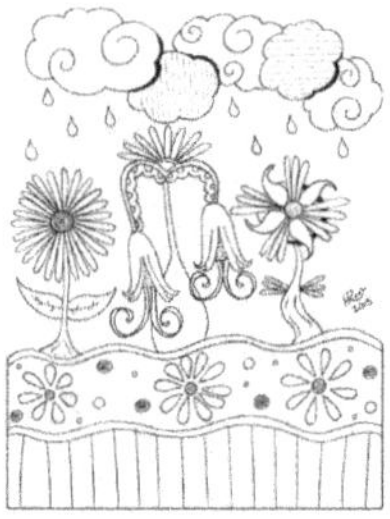

Heather Richards

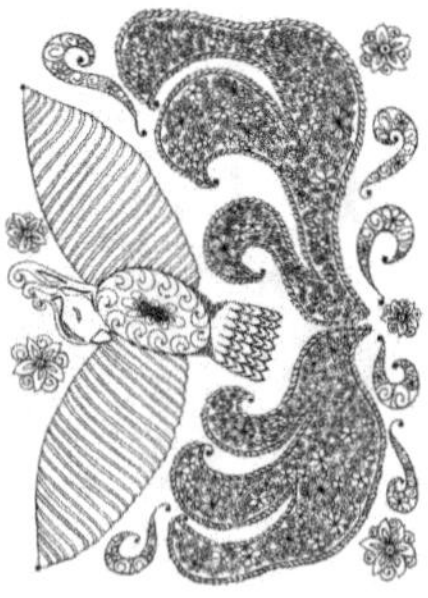

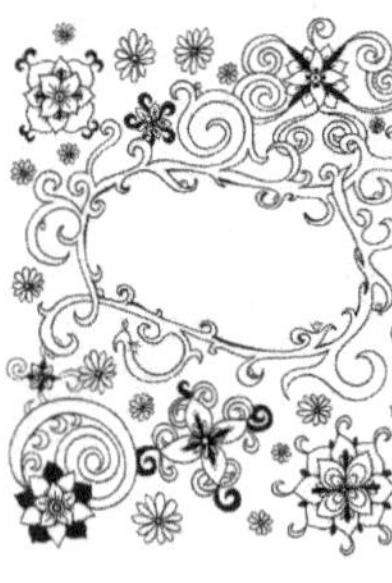

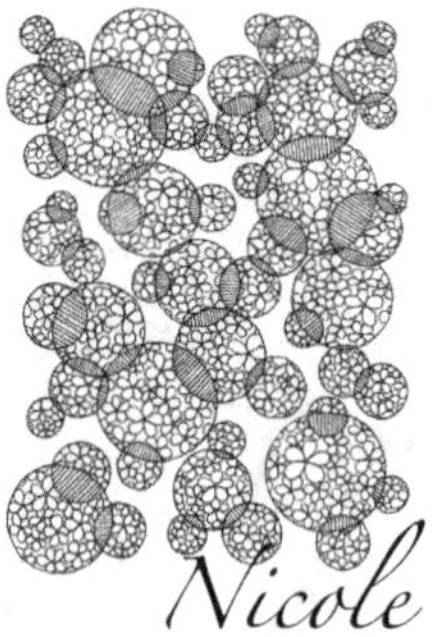

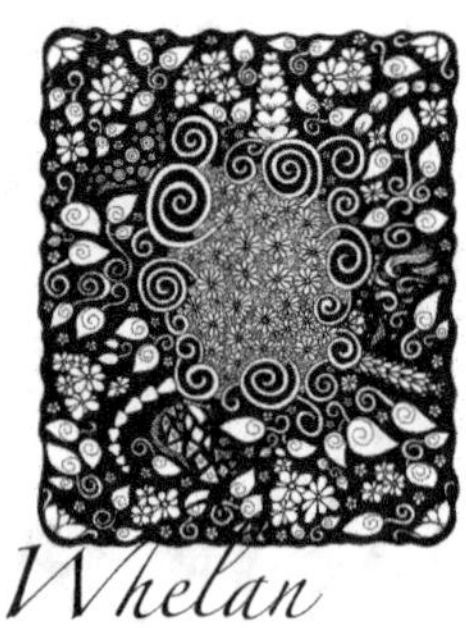

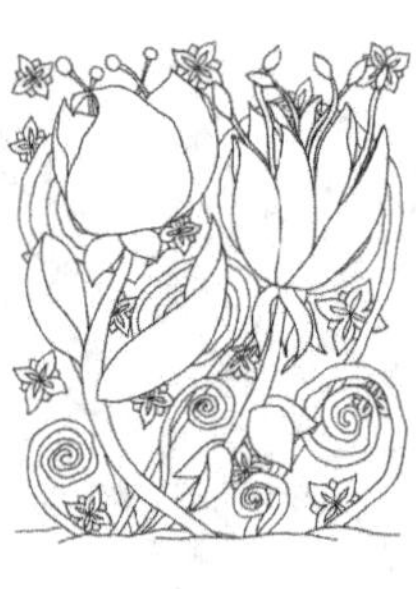

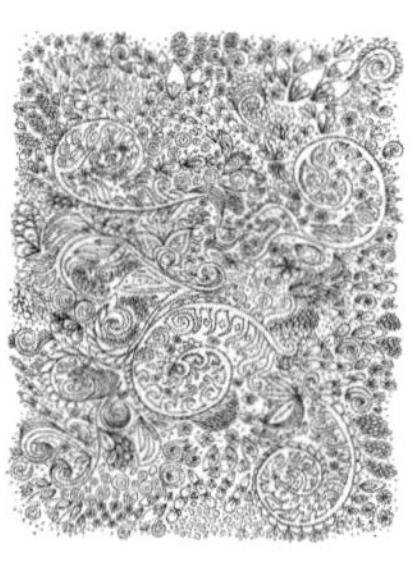

Nicole Whelan

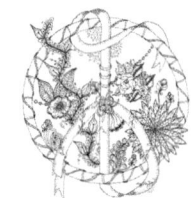
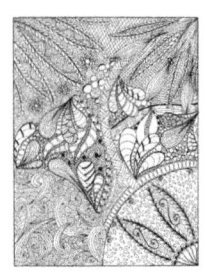
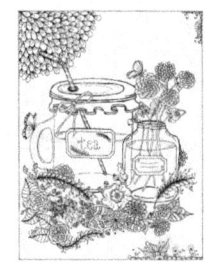
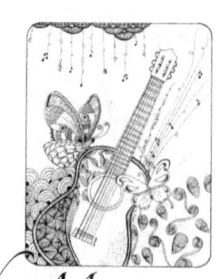
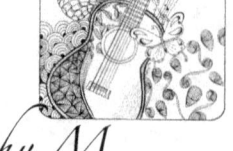
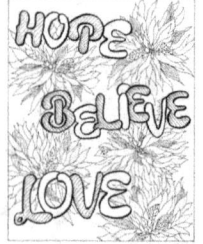
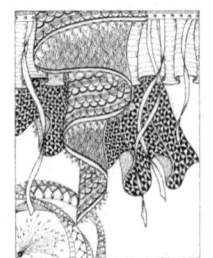

Cathy M.

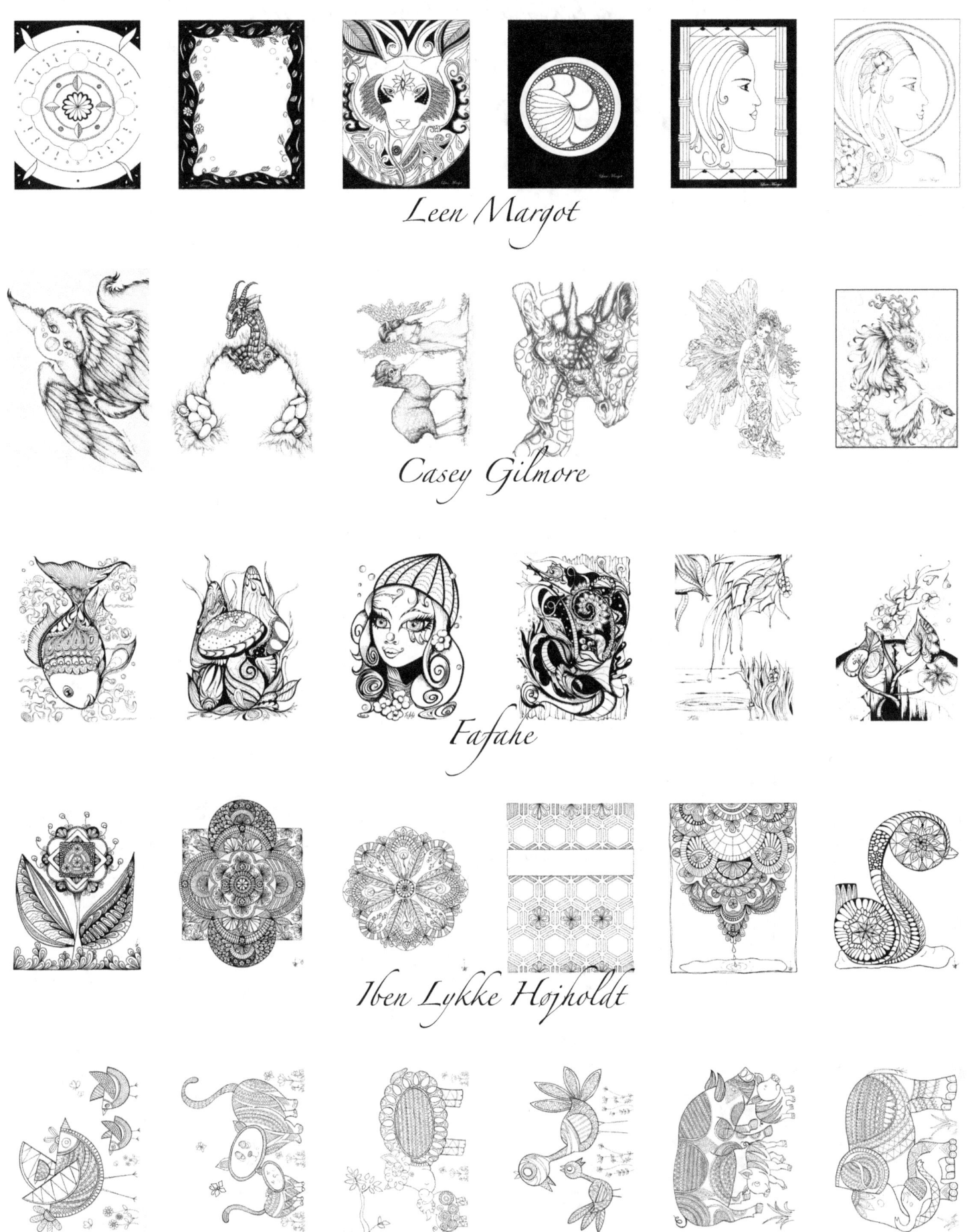

Test your colors here on the samples from
"My Pocket Coloring Companion"
&
"My Coloring Companion"

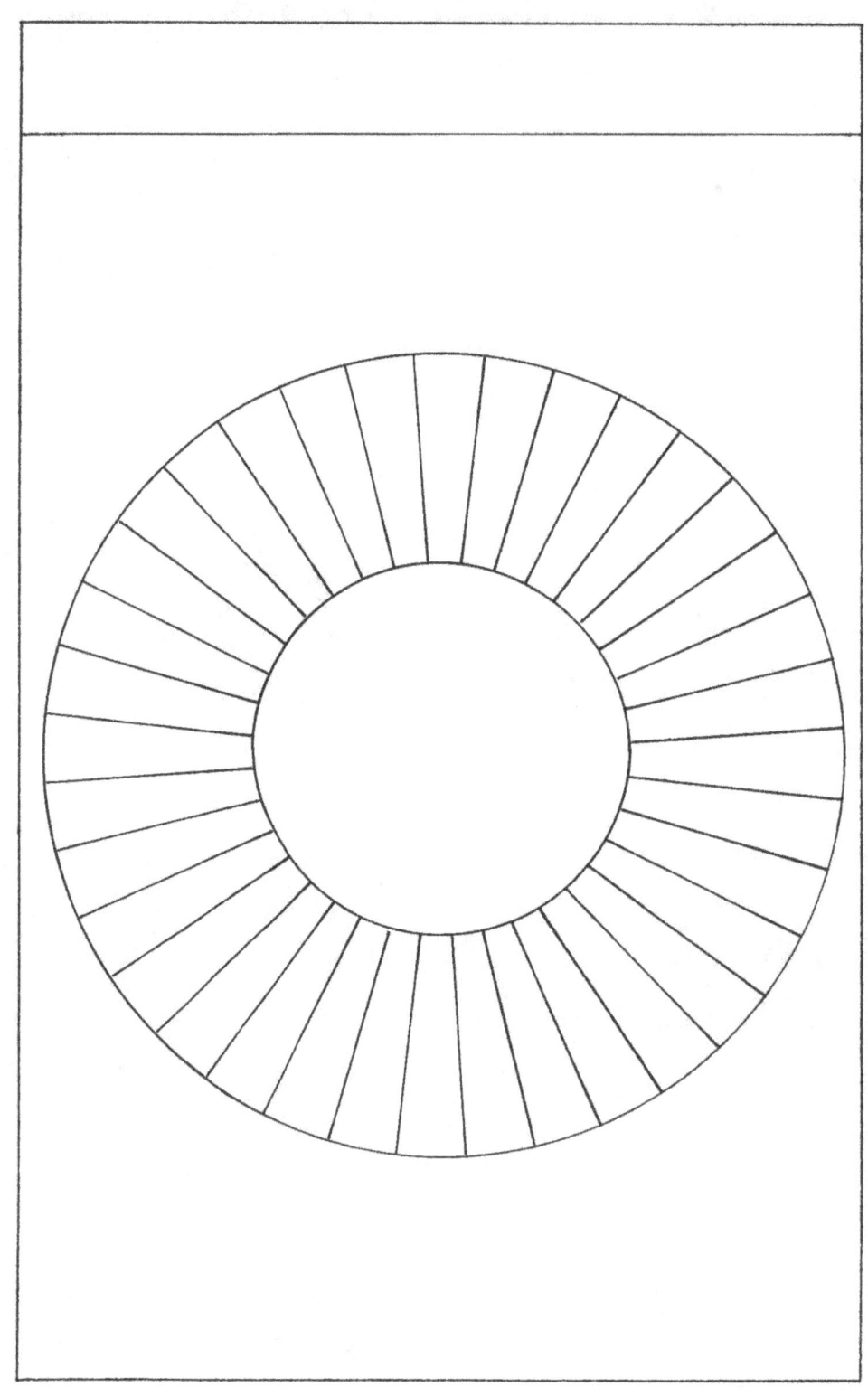

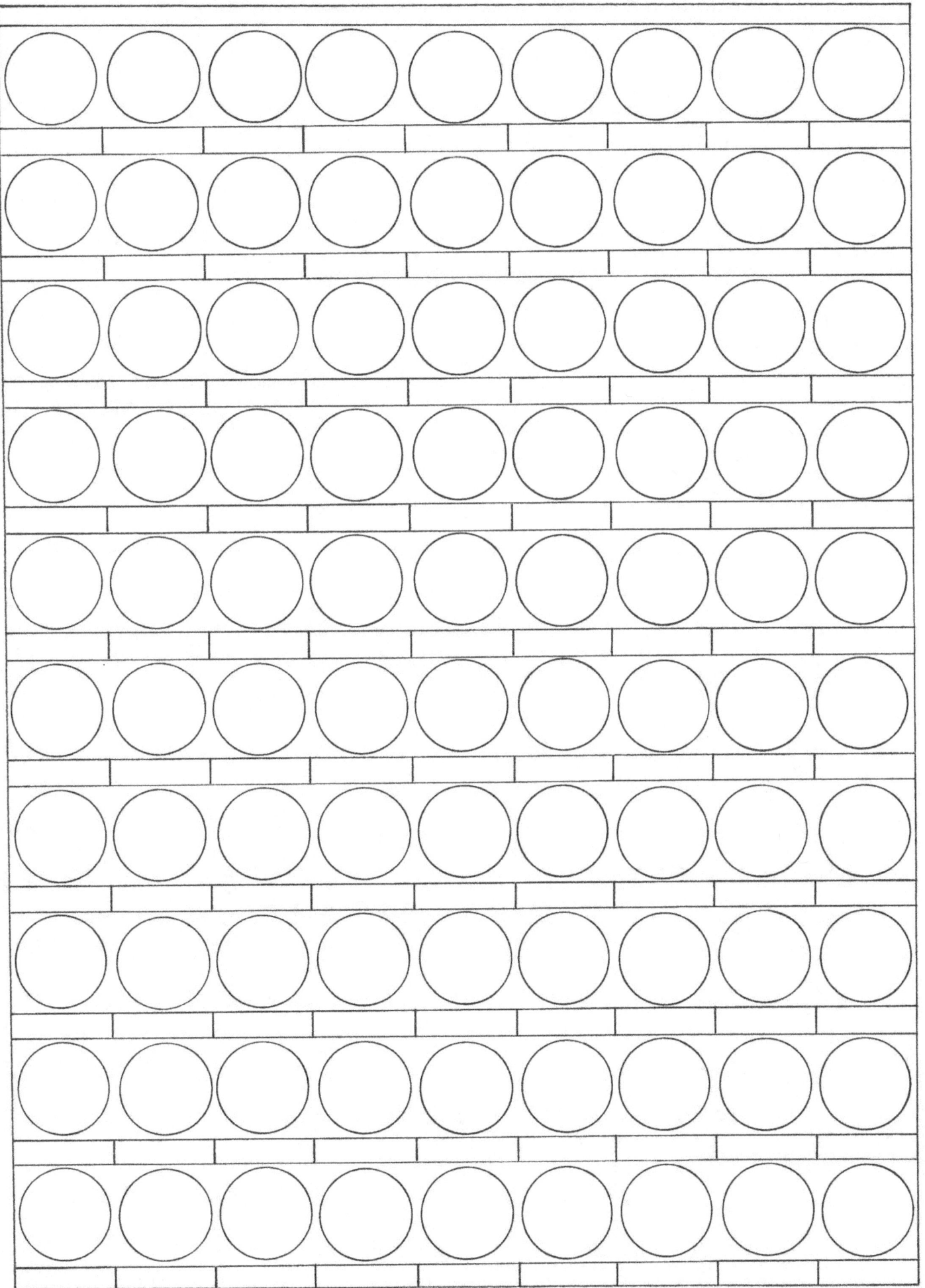

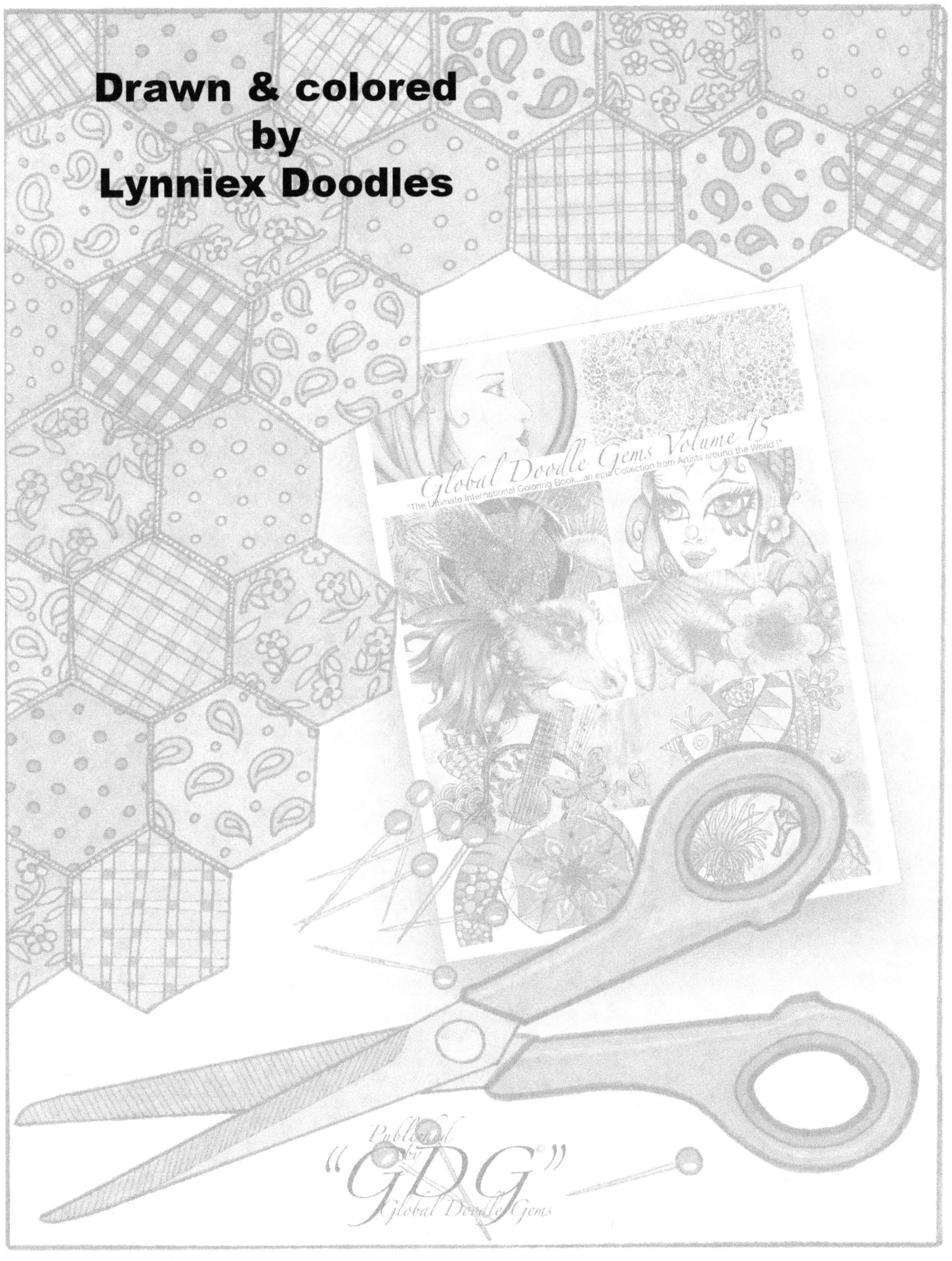

Drawn & colored by Lynniex Doodles

www.ingramcontent.com/pod-product-compliance
Lightning Source LLC
Chambersburg PA
CBHW082207220526
45470CB00010B/3079